RobotBASIC Projects For The Lego NXT

Robot Programming for Beginners

John Blankenship & Samuel Mishal

Copyright © 2011 by
John Blankenship and Samuel Mishal

ISBN-13: 978-1450558570   ISBN-10: 1450558577

Contents AT A Glance

Table Of Contents

Preface

Not long ago, if you wanted to build a robot you needed a degree in electronics. Nowadays, many companies provide motor controllers, sensors, and even kits that make it easy for anyone to experiment with hobby robotics. No one though, makes experimenting with hardware any easier than Lego.

Lego's NXT system allows you to snap together a robot base without tools of any kind. They provide a variety of self-contained, modular sensors and motors that can be interfaced with the NXT computer by simply connecting them with plug-in cables.

The problem with the NXT Robot though is software. While the visual programming language that ships with the system is supposed to be easy-to-use for beginners, many find it far from intuitive. Unless the tasks you are attempting are rudimentary and uncomplicated you may find the NXT's programming system difficult to comprehend. Even many of the after-market languages available for the NXT have cryptic syntax that can frustrate a new user.

One solution to these problems is RobotBASIC. Its easy-to-use English-like syntax makes programming easy to grasp, even for beginners. We provide a library of routines that allow you to control the NXT without downloading *anything* to the robot itself. RobotBASIC controls the NXT's motors and reads sensory data by talking directly to the NXT computer using Lego's wireless protocol. With our system, you program totally on the PC and when your program is ready, just run it and watch the robot respond.

Our Lego Library even has optional (but recommended) predefined constants and conversions that make programming even easier for beginners. You can command the robot to move at a FAST rate, for example, instead of setting the motor speed to an obscure number like 74. As another example of simplicity, our library returns distances measured with the range sensor in inches rather than milliseconds.

We also provide a Lego Simulation Library that allows your NXT programs to operate with the RobotBASIC simulator, letting you experiment even when the Lego hardware is not available.

The Simulation Library is extremely valuable for schools because a robotics curriculum can be implemented with only a single robot per classroom or perhaps even one per school. Every student can work with their own simulated robot both at home and in the classroom and when someone gets their program working, just plugging in a USB Bluetooth adapter will instantly allow their program to control the real NXT.

This system makes programming easier to understand because the user can concentrate on concepts rather than cryptic syntax or an unintuitive graphical interface.

Finally, RobotBASIC is a powerful, full-featured robot-control language, so after you have learned all you can from the NXT you can still use the RobotBASIC skills you learn from this book when you move on to other hardware technologies with more options and capabilities.

Chapter 1

The Lego NXT

The Lego NXT system comes with three gear-head motors and numerous sensors that can be used, along with a multitude of plastic snap-together structural parts, to build a robot. Lego's experiments often create different robots based on the sensors needed at the time. We felt it made more sense to build *one* robot that had all the sensors needed for our experiments.

Our Robot
The robot used throughout this book is shown in Figure 1.1. It uses two motors to move the robot, each motor moving one of the main drive wheels. When both wheels turn the same direction, the robot will move forward or backward. When they move in opposite directions, the robot will rotate left or right.

The Sensors
The robot supports a variety of sensors. A bumper sensor is mounted at the front of the robot to allow it to detect objects in its way. A sound sensor allows it to react to hand claps or other sudden noises.

Figure 1.1: This NXT robot will be used throughout the book.

An ultrasonic ranging sensor measures the distance to objects. This sensor is mounted on a motor controlled turret so that objects can be detected in front of the robot or off to the left side. When facing forward, the ranging sensor can be used to avoid objects blocking the robot's path. When it is faced to the side, it can be used to make the robot remain close to an object so as to navigate around it by following its contour.

Three line sensors are mounted near the front of the robot. Three are used in our robot in order to demonstrate a variety of line following methodologies. If your robot only has one line sensor, don't worry, because projects are provided for that configuration too.

Physical Construction

If you have experimented with a Lego NXT system you will notice that the main body of our robot is basically constructed like one shown in their construction guide. If you have played with any of the Lego parts, you probably will have no trouble modifying Lego's original design so that it can support the additional sensors needed for our projects. Many of our modifications (such as the bumper sensor assembly and the rotating rear wheel) are similar to those shown in various projects in the Lego documentation. If you need more help, Appendix A provides several photos of our robot in various stages of completion. Your robot does not have to be exactly like ours. The important thing is that your robot support all the sensors *you* wish to experiment with.

As you proceed with your construction, there are a few things to keep in mind. The line sensors should be mounted at the front of the robot so that they hang about a quarter of an inch above the ground. The turret motor that moves the range sensor on our model is mounted on the rear of the robot to maintain proper balance. Without the rear weight, the robot can tip forward pushing the line sensors against the ground causing faulty readings.

The rotating turret that positions the ranging sensor works well, but it is far from sophisticated. A simple lever attached to one of the gears acts as a stop at both ends of the turret's rotational travel. To move to either of the two possible positions, we simply turn on the motor briefly (the on-time was arrived at experimentally) in the proper direction after which the motor coasts toward its destination.

The lever easily stops the turret's movement at each end of its travel since the motor is no longer under power. A series of gears (you could also use some form of belt-assembly) allows the drive motor to be mounted on the rear of the robot (for weight balancing, as mentioned earlier) while the ranging sensor is mounted on the front half of the robot. The range sensor needs to be at the front of the robot so it can properly navigate around objects (Chapter 6).

The Lego NXT computer, often referred to as the *brick*, can only control three motors and four sensors simultaneously. Our robot has only three motors so no problems there, but it has six sensors (sound, bumper, range, and three line sensors) all permanently mounted on the robot. Since none of the experiments in this book need more than four sensors, you will only connect the ones needed for the experiment at hand.

Now that you know what our robot will look like, let's move on to the next chapter and find out how to control its motors.

Chapter 2

Controlling the Motors

Normally when you experiment with a Lego robot, you must download your programs to the NXT's computer. In this text, we will use a different approach. Fortunately, Lego provides links in their system software to allow their robot to be controlled over a Bluetooth wireless line using *direct commands*. This feature allows us to control the NXT robot without downloading any programs. In fact, there will be no need to program the NXT computer at all.

Lego Documentation

Lego makes available extensive documentation and technical information on how to utilize their direct commands, but you won't need to know any of these details thanks to our system. We used Lego's documentation to create a library of routines that make it easy for you to control the robot using simple RobotBASIC commands.

We realize though, that some readers may want more information on how the direct commands work, so we provide the full source code for **LegoLibrary.bas** in

Appendix B. We strongly suggest though, that you work through the entire book before you even look at Appendix B. Remember, you don't need *any* of the material in Appendix B to understand any of the projects in this book, so ignore it for now and concentrate on learning the principles of how to program the robot.

RobotBASIC's Direct Command Library

In order to make controlling the robot as easy as possible, we have isolated all the technical complexities in a set of library routines. When the library is *included* in your RobotBASIC programs, you will have available numerous commands that allow you to control motors and read sensory data. Later chapters will explain how to utilize the sensors to create intelligent behaviors. For now, let's see how to control the Lego motors using the library routines. Look at the program shown in Figure 2.1.

```
#include "LegoLibrary.bas"
BluetoothPort = 34
call LegoInit(BluetoothPort)
call LegoDriveMotors(FAST,FAST)
call Wait(3000)
call LegoDriveMotors(STOP,STOP)
end
```

Figure 2.1: This simple program demonstrates how to control two of the Lego NXT's motors.

A Motor Control Demo Program

The program in Figure 2.1 demonstrates how to control the robot's motors, but it also shows how easy it is to use the library routines. *This text assumes you have at least a <u>little</u> programming experience with RobotBASIC*. We will provide nearly everything you need to know, but if you have never programmed with RobotBASIC before, we suggest you go through *Appendix E* and perhaps the *PDF Tutorial* on the home page at **www.RobotBASIC.com**. You can also use the RobotBASIC **HELP File** to obtain more information on commands used in this book. If you have never programmed before in any language, you should consider reading one of our beginner's books such as ***Robots in the Classroom*** or ***RobotBASIC Projects for Beginner's***, both of which are available through our web site.

ⓘRobotBASIC has **two** types of modular structures called *subroutines*. The first of these is the **GOSUB**-style subroutine typicaly used in most dialects of the BASIC language. RobotBASIC also has a more advanced, **CALL**able function-style subroutine that allows for parameter passing and local variables. This book will make extensive use of both of these types of subroutines and it is important that you understand how to use both types. See Appendix F for more information.

The first line in the program of Figure 2.1 causes the **LegoLibrary** to be *temporarily* added to a program when you run it, and then erased when the program terminates. The library file must be in the same directory as your RB program, or you can specify a path with the file name in the **#include** statement.

When the library is included, all the *routines* in the library file will be available to your program just as if you had written them yourself. In this program we will *call* three different library routines to demonstrate how easy this process is. Calling these routines is how we tell them to execute. We can pass information to a routine by listing it between the parentheses following the name of the routine. When the routine finishes its job, it terminates and execution continues with the code following the line with the **call** statement.

> ⓘThe names of the library routines (as well as all variables used in RobotBASIC) are case sensitive. Misspelling a name or using the wrong capitalization will prevent RobotBASIC from finding it. This will cause an error indicating that the name of the desired function is incorrect. The commands in RobotBASIC (things like `call`, `#include`, and so forth) are NOT case sensitive.

LegoInit( )

The first `call` is to a routine called `LegoInit()`. It is assumed you have linked your Lego NXT system to your PC using a Bluetooth adapter. If you are not familiar with how to do this, refer to Appendix C for more information.

When you `call` the `LegoInit()` routine, you must pass it the port number assigned to your connection. Again, refer to Appendix C if you need help with this topic.

On our machine, the Bluetooth connection for the Lego robot was 34. You could place the 34 directly in the call to `LegoInit()`, but we will use a variable as shown in Figure 2.1. The reason for using a variable will become clear later in the book. The `call` to `LegoInit()` automatically establishes communication with the Lego robot and initializes the library so it can be used in your program. Calls to the library routines will cause errors if the library has not been properly initialized.

LegoDriveMotors( )

The next program line calls the `LegoDriveMotors()` routine and passes it two predefined variables. In this case, we are asking both the left and right motors to turn at the **FAST** speed. You can also command each motor to move **SLOW** and **STOP**. Actually, the library lets you specify numerically the exact speeds you want, but you should use the predefined values for everything in this book, because they will allow you to use the simulation library, but more on that later.

The first parameter passed to **LegoDriveMotors()** controls the motor connected to Port 1, which on our robot is the left motor. The second number controls port 2 which should be the right-hand motor.

Once the motors are turned on, the program delays for 3000 ms (3 seconds) by calling a library routine called **Wait**. Finally, another call to **LegoDriveMotors()** turns all motors off.

> ⓘ RobotBASIC has a **delay** command but it should *not* be used with the programs in this book. The **Wait** routine shown in Figure 2.1 provides the same delay, but it also provides added functionalities needed by other library routines.

When you run the program in Figure 2.1, the robot should move forward for three seconds then stop. If the program does not work properly, start by checking to see if your motors are connected to the correct ports. If there is a problem with the Bluetooth connection, RobotBASIC will issue an error saying the port is not available.

Once you get the program running, try replacing both the **FAST** parameters with **SLOW** to make the robot move forward, but at a slower speed. If a parameter is negative, the associated motor will turn in reverse. Two negative numbers will make the robot go backwards. If one number is negative and the other positive, the robot should spin in place, because one wheel is moving forward and the other is moving backward.

Can you guess what would happen if you issued this command:

```
call LegoDriveMotors(SLOW, FAST)
```

Since the right motor will move faster than the left, the robot will move forward, but in a slow turn to the left.

Look at the program in Figure 2.2. It turns the motors on in a particular way then waits a specified number of milliseconds. When the program is run, the robot should move forward about half the length of the robot, then make a left turn of about 90 degrees, then move forward again. If the robot is not making a proper right turn, try adjusting the **Wait** time. A bigger wait time will make the robot turn more, a smaller delay will turn the robot less.

```
#include "LegoLibrary.bas"
BluetoothPort = 34
call LegoInit(BluetoothPort)
call LegoDriveMotors(SLOW, SLOW)
call Wait(1500)
call LegoDriveMotors(-SLOW, SLOW)
call Wait(1100)
call LegoDriveMotors(SLOW, SLOW)
call Wait(1500)
call LegoDriveMotors(STOP, STOP)
end
```

Figure 2.2: This program moves the robot through a specific sequence.

Open-Loop Control

When you control a robot as demonstrated in Figure 2.2, it is called *open-loop* control. This simply means that you tell the robot what to do, but you never get any feedback to let you know if your commands were actually executed successfully. In the chapters that follow, we will begin to learn how information derived from sensors can influence how our robot behaves. The ultimate goal for this text is to help you learn to use this sensory data to implement *closed-loop* feedback systems so that your robot can react to its environment.

More Library Routines

Actions such as moving forward about half the length of the robot and turning 90° come in handy, as we will see in future chapters. Figure 2.3 shows how we could build two routines that perform these actions.

The low-level routines in the Lego Library are function-style **call**able routines because they need parameters to be passed to them. The routines in Figure 2.3 are standard **gosub**-style routines. Appendix F provides information on these two types of subroutines.

The first routine in Figure 2.3 is called **LegoAdvance**. It turns the motors on so as to move the robot forward then waits a predefined time period before turning the motors off. If the **AdvanceTime** is calibrated properly, the robot should move about ½ its length.

```
LegoAdvance:
    call LegoDriveMotors(SLOW, SLOW)
    call Wait(AdvanceTime)
    call LegoDriveMotors(STOP, STOP)
return
//---------------------------------
LegoFaceLeft:
    call LegoDriveMotors(-SLOW, SLOW)
    call Wait(LeftTurnTime)
    call LegoDriveMotors(STOP, STOP)
return
//---------------------------------
LegoHalt:
    call LegoDriveMotors(STOP, STOP)
return
```

Figure 2.3: These routines, when properly calibrated, make the robot move half its length and turn right 90°.

The second routine in Figure 2.3 is **LegoFaceLeft**. It is similar to the **LegoAdvance** routine except that it turns the motors on in opposite directions, making the robot rotate around its center. If the variable **LeftTurnTime** is initialized to an appropriate value, the robot should turn approximately 90°.

The last routine in Figure 2.3 halts the robot by making a call to the **LegoDriveMotors()** routine to stop both motors.

These new routines are easier to use (especially for beginners) than the callable routines used in Figure 2.2 because the new routines do not require you to specify any parameters. For that reason, these routines are also included in the **LegoLibrary**. Look at the program in Figure 2.4. It uses the new routines to perform the same basic actions as the program in Figure 2.2. Notice that you **GOSUB** to these routines instead of **CALL**ing them.

```
#include "LegoLibrary.bas"
BluetoothPort = 34
call LegoInit(BluetoothPort)
gosub LegoAdvance
gosub LegoFaceLeft
gosub LegoAdvance
gosub LegoHalt
end
```

Figure 2.4: This program performs the same actions as Figure 2.2.

Another advantage to using the new routines is that it is easier to see what the program is doing. When you see the statement **gosub LegoFaceLeft** you can guess it will turn the robot to the left even if you don't know how to program. For that reason, we will use routines like these throughout the book.

Additional Routines

In order to make it as easy as possible for beginners, we have provided many routines similar to the ones shown in Figure 2.3. A list of routines that make it easy to control the movement of the Lego robot is shown in Figure 2.5. The figure also explains what each routine does, but, as mentioned earlier, the name of the routine is usually sufficient.

The easy rights and lefts move the robot forward with a gentle turn in the direction indicated. Hard rights and lefts turn quickly with only a little forward movement. These actions were chosen because they can serve as the basis for the more complex behaviors developed in later chapters. When you write programs to control the Lego robot you can freely mix any of the Library routines to accomplish your goal. Just be sure to use the correct statement (**gosub** or **call**) to execute your chosen routines.

ROUTINE NAME	ACTION PERFORMED
LegoAdvance	Forward ½ length of robot
LegoRetreat	Backward ½ length of robot
LegoFaceRight	Right turn 90°
LegoFaceLeft	Left turn 90°
LegoHardRight	Quick turn to the right
LegoEasyRight	Slow turn to the right
LegoHardLeft	Quick turn to the left
LegoEasyLeft	Slow turn to the left
LegoHalt	Stop the robot

Figure 2.5: These library routines make it easy to control the robot's movement.

Calibrating the Routines

These new routines should move your robot as previously described, but no two motors are alike due to differences in friction, efficiency, and other factors. For that reason you should not expect the robot to move exactly half its distance when it advances, nor should you expect it to make perfect right-angle turns. This is typical when an open-loop system is used to control a robot.

The whole purpose of this book is to show you how to use information obtained from the sensors mounted on the robot to make your robot move appropriately and even intelligently. So, at this point, don't worry if your robot is not doing exactly what you think it should do. As long as the movements are reasonable (perhaps a 10-15% error) then we will be able to use the library to create accurate closed-loop behaviors. If your robot's movements are off by large amounts, refer to Appendix D for information on how to calibrate the libraries for your particular robot. Remember, unless your robot has significant errors when it moves, you do not need to perform any calibration at all.

The Lego Simulator

In addition to the **LegoLibrary**, we also have provided a **LegoSimulationLibrary**. The simulation library has all the same functions, but they control the RobotBASIC simulated robot instead of the real Lego robot. To see the simulation in action, use either the program in Figure 2.2 or 2.4, but change the first line in the program to:

```
#include "LegoSimulationLibrary.bas"
```

After you have made the change, run the program. You will see a small circular robot appear on the screen. It will move forward about half its length and then turn to the left and move forward again, just like the real Lego robot did.

If you run the program several times, and watch closely, you will see that the simulated robot does not always move or turn exactly the same amount. It has a slight amount of random error associated with everything it does, just like a real robot. Let's look at an example to demonstrate this point.

Examining the New Movements

Use the program in Figure 2.6 to see how the robot reacts to the new library routines shown in Figure 2.5. Learn to control your robot's movements by modifying the program with different commands. Compare the turning radius with both hard and easy turns to the face right and left commands. With each variation, change the **#include** statement to use the standard **LegoSimulationLibrary** to see how closely the real robot responds like the simulation.

```
#include "LegoLibrary.bas"
BluetoothPort = 34
call LegoInit(BluetoothPort)
gosub LegoEasyRight
call Wait(4000)
gosub LegoHalt
end
```

Figure 2.6: Use the program to experiment
with the new movement routines.

Demonstrating Errors

Look at the program in Figure 2.7. The **for** loop causes
the robot to move forward twice then face right, four times
in a row. Think about this for a moment or perhaps even
try it yourself. Stand in an open room, move forward two
steps, and turn right. Now do this three more times. If you
took exactly the same size steps and turned right exactly
90°, then you would have moved in a square pattern and
returned to your original position.

Remember though, our robot's movements are not
perfect. Enter the program in Figure 2.7 and run it to see
the simulated robot try to move in a square pattern. You
will notice that the simulated robot has an error in its
movement. The error is realistic – run the program several
times and you will see that the robot moves differently each
time. If you change the first line of the program to use the
standard **LegoLibrary**, you will see the real robot move
in a similar manner.

The lines in Figure 2.8 were drawn because of the **call**
to the library routine **LegoPen(DOWN)** in Figure 2.7, which
causes the robot to leave a trail as it moves (as if a pen
mounted at the center of the robot was lowered so it can
draw as the robot moves). You can substitute **UP** with
DOWN to raise the pen if you wish to stop leaving a trail.

```
#include "LegoSimulationLibrary.bas"
BluetoothPort = 34
call LegoInit(BluetoothPort)
call LegoPen(DOWN)
for i=1 to 4
  gosub LegoAdvance
  gosub LegoAdvance
  gosub LegoFaceRight
next
gosub LegoHalt
end
```
Figure 2.7: This program moves the robot in a square pattern.

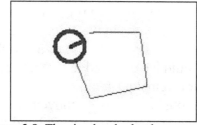

Figure 2.8: The simulated robot has error in its movement, just like a real robot.

You can see from Figure 2.8 that the robot is indeed *trying* to move in a square motion. It is important to realize that even if you could calibrate the library *perfectly*, the robot will still not move in a square because there is always some error added to its actions. We will learn how to overcome this error in future chapters by creating programs that allow our robot to adjust its movements based on its environment. If you are new to robot programming this may sound difficult or even impossible, but it is actually far easier than you might imagine. Roll up your sleeves and move on to the next chapter. The adventure is about to begin.

Chapter 3

The Line Sensor

This chapter introduces many principles and techniques needed in later chapters, so you should study it carefully before moving on.

Recall the exercise in Chapter 2 where you were asked to pretend you were a robot and perform two actions (move forward, turn right), four times in a row. If done perfectly, your movements would describe a square. If you tried it though you know you don't end up exactly where you started and you are facing at least a slightly different direction.

Feedback
If you try these actions with your eyes open you can move in a square easily, because the feedback from your eyes allows you to constantly monitor your motion and continually correct any mistakes. This is a powerful concept and one we should apply to our robot in nearly all situations.

An Algorithm for Following a Line
In order to demonstrate this principle we will develop an *algorithm* (a step-by-step plan) for our robot to follow. Coming up with an appropriate algorithm is not always easy so let's examine how it can be done.

For this example, we will assume that our robot has a single line sensor mounted near its front bumper. The sensor generates a value of 1 (meaning it is over a black line) or 0 (meaning it sees only white space). These sensors work by emitting light towards the ground and then using a photo-detector to determine if the light is reflected back. A light colored surface reflects the light and a dark surface does not. An easy way to create our line is to draw it with a black felt-tip marker on a white poster board.

The easiest way for you to develop an algorithm is to place yourself in the position of the robot. In this example, the robot is being asked to follow a line but it only has one "eye" and can only see a tiny little area below the sensor. To give you the same limitation as the robot, cut a small hole in a 3 by 5 card and lay it on the line as shown in Figure 3.1.

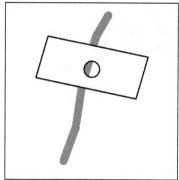

Figure 3.1: The hole in the card lets you see the line the way the robot does.

In order to make this experiment even more like the robot, get a friend to help you. One of you will be the robot program that decides what to do, and the other person will be the sensor and the motors of the robot – we will call that person the hardware-person.

Assume a starting position where the line can be seen through the hole. The hardware-person says "I see the line" and the program person must decide what to do. For instance she may say "Move forward" or "Turn right" or other similar actions. After the hardware-person moves the card in the manner requested, he acts like the sensor and reports whether the line can be seen or not. Using this new information, the program-person has to decide on the new action.

If you think about this for a moment, it should be obvious that the program-person only has two actions that can be ordered; one action if a line is seen and another action if a line is not seen. Get a 3 by 5 card and another person to help and see if you can figure out what actions should be taken when the line is seen and not seen. Remember, the program-person must sit well away from the line so she cannot see it. The only information she has is what is reported by the hardware-person. Please try this exercise before reading the answer below.

The Answer
The answer may be easier than you think. Basically, if we see the line we want to move away from it, always in the same direction (let's say we move forward and right). If we don't see the line, we move back toward it (perhaps forward and left). We can't just move left and right, because that would mean the robot would just sit in one spot and rotate back and forth. The idea behind this solution is that the robot is constantly moving to the right away from the line if it sees it, and back to the left when it can't. Using our two-person experiment, see if this simple algorithm works using a real line and the 3 by 5 card. Once you see that it does work, we are ready to convert this idea into a program.

Converting the Algorithm into a Program
Figure 3.2 shows the code that implements the algorithm described above. The main **while**-loop does all the work. It uses a call to the function **LegoLineSensor()** to read the status of the sensor. There are two parameter passed to

the subroutine. The 2 indicates which Lego Port the sensor is plugged into. The variable **a** is passed so that the routine can place the answer in it. After the call, the variable **a** will be a 1 if a line is seen or 0 otherwise. A multi-line **if**-statement checks the value of **a** and if the line is seen, the library routine **LegoEasyRight** is used to move the robot forward with a drift to the right. If the line is not seen (the **ELSE** block), the robot moves forward with a drift to the left. The loop causes this action to be repeated, thus implementing our algorithm. Notice that both **call** and **gosub** statements are used depending on the type of library routine being executed.

```
#include "LegoSimulationLibrary.bas"
BluetoothPort = 34
gosub DrawLine
call LegoInit(BluetoothPort)
call LegoLineInit(2)
while true
  call LegoLineSensor(2,a)
  if a=1
    gosub LegoEasyRight
  else
    gosub LegoEasyLeft
  endif
wend
end
```

Figure 3.2: This program allows the robot to follow a line using one line sensor.

Initialization

There are three actions that are needed before we are ready to actually execute the loop that implements our algorithm. First, we need to draw a line. In order to make it easy to experiment with our simulation, we included a **DrawLine** subroutine in the library. Simply call it to create the environment shown in Figure 3.3. The **DrawLine()** function only works when the Simulation library is used. A call to this function is simply ignored by the standard library. Of course, when you use the real robot, you will have to provide a real line.

It is also necessary to initialize the **LegoLibrary** just as we have in previous programs. Notice that since we are using a line sensor, we also have to initialize it with a call to **LegoLineInit()**. We must tell the line-sensor initialization module which port on the Brick the sensor is connected to. In this example, we used port 2.

Notice that the program in Figure 3.2 includes the **LegoSimulationLibrary** which causes the algorithm to be carried out with the simulated robot. When the program is run, Figure 3.2 shows the path that the robot takes as it tries to follow the line.

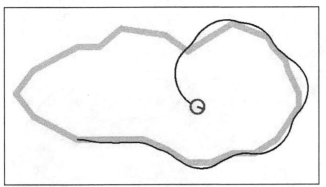

Figure 3.3: The library contains a function to draw a line.

If the line turns too sharply, the robot cannot stay with it and strays from the line, but eventually makes its way back. If the robot ever crosses to the left side of the line (as it does in Figure 3.3) it continues to turn left trying to find the line again – just as the program directs it to do. Of course this action shows a flaw in our algorithm. The robot's behavior is fine as long as the line it is expected to follow does not curve too quickly, but it fails when the line makes a sharp turn.

When you run the program, your robot might lose the line at a totally different spot. This is true because the random error (to create realism) introduced in our library will make every run of the program slightly different.

> ⓘ On the real robot you can use any ports you wish for the various sensors. On the simulation the port numbers used for line sensors will control which of the three simulated line sensors is used. The middle sensor is Port 2, the sensor on the right is Port 1, and Port 3 activates the left sensor.

Possible Solutions

One possible solution to our robot loosing the line is to make the line wider, or even create a solid object and let the robot follow the edge of the object rather than thinking of it as a line. If you think about it, this is actually what our algorithm is doing. When the robot sees the object it moves away and when it doesn't it moves back towards it.

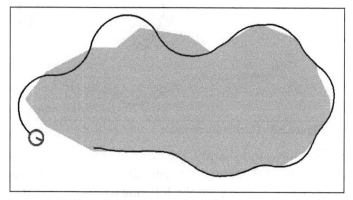

Figure 3.4: The robot can hug close to the edges of a solid object.

Figure 3.4 shows the robots behavior if the object is made solid. Now, when the robot ventures too far left, it still sees the object and knows it should turn to the right. The program now works better, but the robot exhibits a loopy behavior on sharp turns.

Other Solutions

Another possible solution is to make the robot turn quicker instead of those slow lazy drifts to the right and left. This can be done by changing the code as shown in Figure 3.5. The lines that were changed are shown in bold. The robot is made to turn more quickly by stopping the wheel on the turn side instead of just slowing it down.

With the changes shown in Figure 3.5, the robot follows the line almost perfectly, as shown in Figure 3.6. There is an unfortunate side effect though. The quick turns made by the robot make the robot oscillate erratically back and forth as it follows the line.

```
#include "LegoSimulationLibrary.bas"
BluetoothPort = 34
gosub DrawLine
call LegoInit(BluetoothPort)
call LegoLineInit(2)
while true
  call LegoLineSensor(2,a)
  if a=1
    gosub LegoHardRight
  else
    gosub LegoHardLeft
  endif
wend
end
```

Figure 3.5: The robot can handle sharp turns if it turns more quickly itself, but now there is an erratic movement.

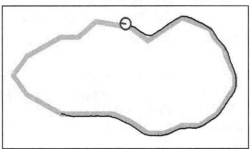

Figure 3.6: This is the path created by the program in Figure 3.5.

Running these programs and studying the robot's behavior can give you a better understanding of our algorithm, which will be valuable as we strive to improve on it in later chapters. It can also help you understand the deficiencies such as the wobbly movement associated with using fast turns. There is an important aspect of this discussion that needs to be emphasized. We have learned many powerful ideas and concepts about a robot following a line, and yet we have not utilized a real robot at all.

Simulations are used in many industries (not just robotics) to solve problems and explore solutions without the time and expense of using real hardware. Once solutions are found, they can then be applied to real-world situations. Depending on how accurate the simulations are, the final programs may have to be modified to fine tune the final behaviors, but that is far easier than developing the entire algorithm on real-world hardware.

Moving to the Real-World

The next step is to see how closely our simulator emulates the real world. Try running the programs of Figure 3.2 and 3.5 but change the first line to include the standard **LegoLibrary.bas** instead of the simulation one. Of course, if you are going to use the real robot, you will need a real line for the robot to follow as shown in Figure 3.7. Notice we have (starting at the bottom of the photo) a curvy line, a nearly straight line, and a circular line similar to what was used with the simulation. The lines were drawn with a black felt tip marker on white poster board. To keep the real line proportional to the size of the simulated line (compared to the spacing of the simulated sensors) the real line should be about one and three-quarter inches wide. If the spacing for the real line and the simulated line are not similar, you cannot expect the two robots to react in the same manner.

The program shown in Figure 3.2 should only follow a fairly straight line without losing it. The program in Figure

3.5 will follow all the lines shown, and it does so with the erratic wobble predicted by the simulation.

Figure 3.7: You must create lines for the real robot to follow.

Reducing the Speed

Another option for improving the robot's ability to follow the line is to reduce its speed. This will reduce the wobble effect demonstrated by the program in Figure 3.5 and the slower movement will help prevent the program in Figure 3.2 from losing the line when it curves too quickly.

Appendix C provides information on customizing the libraries, thus allowing you to control the speed of the robot as well as many other parameters. Unless your robot is not following the line properly, there is no reason to introduce confusing options but it is valuable to know that such options exist.

A Debugging Option

When a program is not producing the expected results, it becomes necessary to debug your code. For those readers not familiar with debugging techniques, we recommend studying the RobotBASIC HELP file as well as our introductory programming books (mentioned in Chapter 1).

In addition to all of RobotBASIC's standard debugging tools, we have added a special feature to the Lego Libraries. Just add the following line immediately after you call **LegoInit()** to enable debugging.

```
LegoDebug = TRUE
```

This will cause your program to *pause* every time *any* sensor function is called and wait for you to press the ENTER key. In our program, for example, the program will stop when **LegoLineSensor()** is called. At that point, the robot (either the real robot or the simulation, depending on which Library you are using) will automatically stop moving and the RobotBASIC terminal screen will display something similar to Figure 3.8.

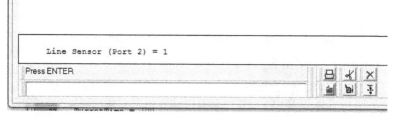

Figure 3.8: Both Lego Libraries have this special debugging feature.

As you can see from the figure, the sensor being interrogated will be displayed, as well as its current reading. In this example, we know that the robot is currently seeing a line because the line sensor has a value of 1. Knowing that, you should be able to predict what action the program should take. When you press the ENTER key, the robot will make its next move and stop again when a sensor function is called. If the robot does not move as expected you have one additional clue as to what might be wrong with your algorithm or your implementation of it.

This debugging feature can help you (or students) understand how an algorithm works (especially nice for teachers). It can also provide insights on how to improve on an algorithm you are trying to develop because it helps you see specific sensor conditions that are not being handled properly. We will examine these principles more in later chapters.

Summary
This chapter introduced many principles you will need in future chapters. Our next step is to learn how to utilize the data from the sound, bumper, and range sensors. Once you have a good grasp of how sensors can be used, we will create programs that utilize multiple sensors to give the robot more intelligent behaviors.

Chapter 4

The Sound Sensor

Now that you understand the basics of reading a sensor and using its data to control the behavior of your robot, we are ready to examine how to use the other sensors on our Lego robot. This chapter introduces the sound sensor. The Lego sound sensor is basically a microphone connected in a manner that allows the computer to detect the amount of sound it hears.

Initializing the Sound Sensor

We can initialize the sound sensor using the library routine `LegoSoundInit()`. This routine only has to be called once at the beginning of your program to prepare the sound sensor for use. As with the line sensor, another routine, `LegoSoundSensor()`, will actually be used to read information from the sensor.

We can use the library routine `LegoSoundSensor()` to detect sudden changes in sounds such as a hand clap or the dropping of something on the floor.

A Sound Sensor Demo Program

The program in Figure 4.1 demonstrates how to read the sound sensor and move the robot slightly forward each time a sound occurs.

```
#include "LegoLibrary.bas"
BluetoothPort = 34
SoundPort = 3  // set to the port you use
call LegoInit(BluetoothPort)
call LegoSoundInit(SoundPort)
while true
  call LegoSoundSensor(SoundPort,50,s)
  if s then gosub LegoAdvance
wend
end
```

Figure 4.1: This program moves the robot when a sound is heard.

At the beginning of the program in Figure 4.1, we set a variable called **SoundPort** equal to the number of the port where your sound sensor is attached (1-4). This variable is not necessary, but certainly recommended. You could have just used the actual number throughout the program, but this way, if you move the sensor to a different port, you only need to change one line in the program.

Next we initialize the library with a call to **LegoInit()**, passing it the Bluetooth port number. Then we initialize the sound sensor itself.

A **while-wend** loop repeats everything inside it until the expression following the **while** is **false**. Since the expression is set to **true**, the loop never stops.

Inside the **while**-loop we call **LegoSoundSensor()**. Notice we pass it three parameters. The first is the port number used by the sound sensor. The second parameter controls the sensitivity of the port. It can be any number from 0 to 150. Numbers near the bottom of this range force the sensor to be sensitive to even the slightest noise. As the numbers approach 150 you will need a louder sound to trigger the sensor.

The third parameter passed to **LegoSoundSensor()** is the name of the variable you want to hold the sound information. After the call to **LegoSoundSensor()**, this variable will indicate if a sound was detected. If it is

TRUE, then a sound that exceeded the specified sensitivity was detected.

When the variable is TRUE, the **IF-THEN**-statement (a single-line version of the **IF-ELSE-ENDIF** used in Chapter 3) causes the robot to advance a short distance. (Note: The statement following the **THEN** is only executed if the expression in the **IF** is true.

Of course, you can have the robot respond any way you wish when a sound is detected, but this example shows how to use the sound sensor in your own programs.

Using the Simulation
If you change the first line in the program to include the Simulation library (**LegoSimulationLibrary.bas**) instead of the standard one, the simulation robot will respond like the real robot. Since the simulation cannot detect sounds, the library assumes you will hold down the left mouse button to simulate a sound.

Debugging the Sound Sensor
You can use the debug mode with either the real robot or the simulation by adding the following line immediately after the call to **LegoInit()**.

```
LegoDebug = true
```

When you do this, it becomes impossible to detect sounds or even the mouse button (during simulation) so an alternative approach is used. When the sound sensor is interrogated, you are requested to enter a 0 (for no sound) or a 1 (indicating a sound was detected) and then press ENTER (as you always do when debugging). Try using the debug mode with both the real robot and the simulation.

Chapter 5

The Bumper Sensor

O ur robot's bumper physically triggers a Lego switch sensor. The bumper allows our robot to determine when it bumps into an object.

Initializing the Bumper Sensor

All of the Lego sensors need to be initialized just like we did with the sound and line sensors. Use the routine `LegoBumperInit()` to initialize the bumper sensor.

After the bumper sensor has been initialized, the routine `LegoBumperSensor()` can be used to determine when a collision has occurred. We pass it only two parameters since there is no sensitivity setting. The bumper is either pressed or not.

A Bumper Demo Program

The program in Figure 5.1 demonstrates how the bumper can be used. The robot's behavior generated by this program is simple: when the robot encounters an object it turns around a random amount, but something close to 180°.

```
#include "LegoLibrary.bas"
BluetoothPort = 34
BumperPort = 4
call LegoInit(BluetoothPort)
call LegoBumperInit(BumperPort)
while true
  call LegoBumperSensor(BumperPort,b)
  if b
    call LegoDriveMotors(SLOW, -SLOW)
    call Wait(1500 + random(800))
  else
    call LegoDriveMotors(SLOW, SLOW)
  endif
wend
end
```

Figure 5.1: This program causes the robot to
turn away from objects it encounters.

The program in Figure 5.1 should not require much
explanation because it is very similar to the demo for the
sound sensor. When the variable **b** is true, we know the
bumper is pressed, and the robot turns away from the
object. Notice how RobotBASIC's **random()** function
allows the turn time to be between 1500 and 2300
milliseconds. When **b** is false we know that no object is
detected, so a call to **LegoDriveMotors()** keeps the robot
moving forward until an object is encountered. Notice this
action allows the value of the bumper to be checked much
more often than if the **LegoAdvance** routine was used. (If
LegoAdvance were used, the bumper would only be
checked after the robot had moved about ½ its length.)

Debugging the Bumper

If you set **LegoDebug** to TRUE immediately after the call
to **LegoInit()**, the robot will assume its debugging
behavior. Every time a call is made to read the bumper
sensor, the robot will stop and print the status of the
bumper on the RobotBASIC terminal screen. When you
press ENTER, the robot will continue its behavior until

another sensor reading is requested. Add the line to turn debugging on and watch the results. Every time you press ENTER the robot will advance slightly unless it has encountered an object. At that point, pressing ENTER will cause the robot to rotate a random amount away from the object.

Using the Simulation

Change the first line in the program to include the simulation library and you will see the simulated robot respond in a similar manner to the real robot. Try the simulation in the debug mode too. The robot will see the edges of the terminal screen as walls, but you can also draw objects in the room using RobotBASIC's graphics commands such as LINE, CIRCLE, RECTANGLE, etc.

Using Two Sensors

Notice that the robot never turns off when running the program in Figure 5.1 (unless you are debugging). It is always moving forward or turning away from an object. We could use the sound sensor to change this behavior.

At this point, let's see if you understand what you have learned. Try to modify the program in Figure 5.1 so that it turns away from objects just as it does now, but have your robot stop if it hears a sound, and to remain stopped until another sound occurs. At that point, the robot should revert to its original behavior of avoiding objects, until another sound is detected.

Don't read much further until you have tried to create the new program. If you have trouble, you may need more background in programming so consider reading one of our beginner's books. Remember, this book teaches you how to control the Lego robot, but it assumes you already understand some fundamental programming principles.

The New Program

If you have given the above assignment your best effort, and still had some trouble, perhaps looking at a possible solution can help you improve your programming abilities.

Notice, we said a *possible* solution, not *the* solution. Writing a program is similar, in some ways, to writing a novel. Two people could write the same story and yet write it in totally different ways. The same is true when writing a program. Figure 5.2 shows one solution, but do not regard it as the only way to accomplish the goal. Examine it to see how it was done and then use those ideas when you write programs of your own.

The modified program is actually very much like the one in Figure 5.1. The only changes are shown in Figure 5.2 in **bold**.

Some of the changes made to the program are obvious. You must set up a port number for the sound sensor and you must initialize it. The remaining changes are perhaps, not so obvious.

At the end of the original loop several statements have been added. First, the sound sensor is checked and if a sound has been detected, a **repeat-until** loop is entered. The sound sensor is read again inside this loop and the loop continues until it hears a sound. Notice how this causes the behavior we want. The original loop causes the original object-avoidance behavior unless a sound occurs. When it does, the second loop forces the program to wait for a sound before execution of the first loop can continue again.

Study the program in Figure 5.2 carefully. Your goal should be to understand the logic. Make sure that you see why the program performs the original behavior until a sound is detected and why the program waits for a second sound after one has been detected.

```
#include "LegoLibrary.bas"
BluetoothPort = 34
BumperPort = 4
SoundPort = 3
call LegoInit(BluetoothPort)
call LegoBumperInit(BumperPort)
call LegoSoundInit(SoundPort)
while true
  call LegoBumperSensor(BumperPort,b)
  if b
    gosub LegoRetreat
    call LegoDriveMotors(SLOW,- SLOW)
    call Wait(1500 + random(800))
  else
    call LegoDriveMotors(SLOW, SLOW)
  endif
  call LegoSoundSensor(SoundPort,50,s)
  if s
    gosub LegoHalt
    repeat
      call LegoSoundSensor(SoundPort,50,s)
    until s
  endif
wend
end
```

Figure 5.2: The bold lines in this program change it so that a hand clap can be used to start and stop the robot's obstacle avoidance behavior.

Chapter 6

The Range Sensor

The last chapter introduced the bumper sensor as a way for your robot to detect objects. While a bumper can be effective in some situations, the robot must actually make contact with the obstacle to detect it. This chapter will examine a way to detect objects without making physical contact.

Lego's Range Sensor

One solution is Lego's ultrasonic range sensor. It is composed of two transducers, one acting as a speaker, the other as a microphone. It uses the speaker to project a high frequency sound (above the range of human hearing) away from the robot. Then it waits for the sound to strike an object and bounce back to be picked up by the microphone. The time it takes for the sound to return to the robot can be used to calculate the distance to the object.

Measuring the Distance to Objects

The range sensor must be initialized like the other Lego sensors. We do that with the function **LegoRangeInit()** and use **LegoRangeSensor()** to actually read the data, as shown in Figure 6.1. The data provided by the sensor is actually the time for the sound to return, but our library automatically converts it to inches for you. Even the simulation library converts the pixel distances provided by the simulated range sensor into an inch-equivalent so that programs written for the simulation work with the real robot and vice versa. The simulated robot is assumed to be approximately six inches in diameter.

```
#include "LegoLibrary.bas"
BluetoothPort = 34
RangePort = 3
call LegoInit(BluetoothPort)
call LegoRangeInit(RangePort)
while true
   call LegoRangeSensor(RangePort,r)
   xyString 100,150,r," inches   "
wend
end
```

Figure 6.1: This program displays the distance measured by the range sensor.

If you run the program in Figure 6.1 it will display the distance from the front of the robot to the object. Move an object in front of the robot and vary its distance and compare the actual distance with the one displayed on the screen. Angled objects may reflect the sound away from the robot and cause faulty readings. If there are any distance discrepancies you can calibrate the reading by adjusting the formula in the library (see Appendix C).

Using Range Data to Control the Robot

Remember the program in Figure 5.1 from the last chapter. It caused the robot to roam randomly around the room by having it turn away a random amount when it bumped into an object. Test your programming skills by modifying that program so that it works with the range sensor. We want the robot to behave basically the same as before, but instead of colliding with obstacles, it should turn away from objects a few inches before contact is actually made.

Try your best to create this program on your own before moving on to see a possible solution. Figure 6.2 shows one way of accomplishing this task.

```
#include "LegoLibrary.bas"
 BluetoothPort = 34
 RangePort = 3
 call LegoInit(BluetoothPort)
 call LegoRangeInit(RangePort)
 while true
   call LegoRangeSensor(RangePort,r)
   print r
   if r<5
     call LegoDriveMotors(SLOW, -SLOW)
     call Wait(1500 + random(800))
   else
     call LegoDriveMotors(SLOW, SLOW)
   endif
 wend
 end
```

Figure 6.2: This program causes the robot to turn away from objects it encounters, before it touches them.

Looking Left and Ahead

Recall that our robot has the third Lego motor mounted so it can move the range sensor to one of two positions. We have provided two routines in our library for positioning the turret. A **gosub LegoLookAhead** moves the range sensor so it is pointing forward and the routine **LegoLookLeft** rotates the sensor so it points to the left. Both these routines simply turn the motor on for a short time and let it coast toward its final destination. A lever (see the pictures in Appendix A) mounted on one of the gears prevents the turret from moving past either of its final positions.

The speed of the motor and the amount of time it runs is significant. If the motor is turned on too slow or for too short a time it will not reach its intended position. If the motor is too fast or turned on too long, the lever or other robot part might be torn from its mounting. Finding the proper times and speeds may seem like a difficult task, but after only a few tries, acceptable values were found.

Now that we know the range-related functions available to us, it is time to create a program that can demonstrate how the functions can be used. We have learned many skills and principles in previous chapters, so perhaps it is time to make our robot a little more intelligent.

Find a Wall and Follow it

For this project we will teach our robot how to find a wall and then follow that wall for a specified distance. This behavior is handy for many applications. For example, it can be used to find a way out of a maze, or a way around an object blocking the robot's path.

A Complex Project

This project is more complicated than the ones in previous chapters. Part of the reason for this is that there are many new programming principles introduced. For that reason, it is suggested that you take your time and study every aspect of this program. If you understand it completely you will be on your way to becoming a robot programmer.

One of the new principles that we will introduce with this program is modularization. You are already familiar with modular programming; each of our library routines is a module that handles a specific task for us. The point we want to make is that *any* time a program gets complicated, you should consider breaking it down into separate modules that carry out a portion of the entire task. Doing this makes the program easier to understand, easier to create, and easier to debug.

For example, the goal we described for our robot can easily be broken down into two sub-tasks, finding the wall, and following the wall. If we assume we have modules to handle these tasks, then the main part of our program is greatly simplified as you can see in Figure 6.3.

```
Main:
  #include "LegoLibrary.bas"
  BluetoothPort = 34
  RangePort = 3
  call LegoInit(BluetoothPort)
  call LegoRangeInit(RangePort)
  gosub FindWall
  call FollowWall(5) // follow for 5 feet
end
```

Figure 6.3: This program directs the robot to find
a wall and follow it for about five feet.

Notice how modular programming techniques make the logic of the program easy to follow. After some initialization, the robot moves to find a wall then follows the wall for about five feet. The next step, of course, is to create the modules that do the actual work. Notice also, that we used a simple **gosub**-style routine to find the wall because it did not need any parameters passed to it. On the other hand, a function-style routine was used for **FollowWall()** so we can easily specify how far the wall should be followed.

Finding a Wall

The subroutine in Figure 6.4 shows how to make the robot move forward until it detects a wall. It starts by turning the range sensor to the forward position. Next, a **repeat-until** loop takes a range-sensor reading and turns the motors on at an appropriate speed (the robot slows down when it gets within a foot of the wall). This continues until a wall (or other object) is detected at a close range (less than six inches). Of course, you could just move the robot toward the wall at a single speed, but teaching it how to adjust its speed based on its environment can make it seem more intelligent.

When the distance to the wall becomes less than 6 inches, the robot faces to the right and returns to the main program. It is important to remember that since **gosub**-style routines use global variables that this routine can access variables like **SLOW** and **RangePort** without complication.

```
FindWall:
  gosub LookAhead
  repeat
    call LegoRangeSensor(RangePort,r1)
    if r1 > 10
      call LegoDriveMotors(FAST,FAST)
    else
      call LegoDriveMotors(SLOW,SLOW)
    endif
  until r1 < 6
  gosub LegoFaceRight
return
```

Figure 6.4: This subroutine moves the robot forward until it finds a wall.

Following the Wall

Our routine to follow the wall (shown in Figure 6.5) is slightly more complicated than the one used to find the wall. First of all, the new routine is a function-style routine that allows us to pass the number of feet we want the wall to be followed, thus making the routine more flexible.

The first thing our routine does is make the distance sensor point to the left (towards the wall). Our robot will follow the wall by simply trying to stay the same distance from it. In order for this principle to work, the sensor should be pointed about 70° to the left as shown in Figure 6.6. If the robot turns to the left the distance to the wall will decrease and if the robot turns to the right the distance will increase. Notice that this would not be true if the sensor points directly to the left. In that case, the distance to the wall would increase if the robot turned either right or left.

```
sub FollowWall(dist)
  gosub LegoLookLeft
  if _LegoSimulation
    m = dist*700
  else
    m = dist*20
  endif
  for i=1 to m
    call LegoRangeSensor(_RangePort,R)
    if R < 10
      // move away from wall
      gosub LegoEasyRight
    else
      // move closer to wall
      gosub LegoEasyLeft
    endif
  next
  gosub LegoHalt
return
```

Figure 6.5: This subroutine allows the robot to follow a wall.

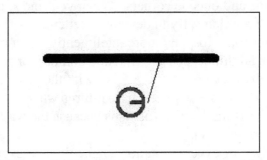

Figure 6.6: For wall following, the distance sensor should point about 70° to the left as shown by the line in front of the robot.

Another important point about Figure 6.6 is that the robot should start with an orientation that is fairly parallel with the wall. If the robot is headed towards the wall, the distance measured would be long, causing the robot to think it was too far from the wall thus making it turn to the left. This is the reason the last line in the **FindWall** routine of Figure 6.5 turned the robot to the right with a **gosub LegoFaceRight**.

The **for**-loop in Figure 6.5 causes the robot to follow the wall for a distance proportional to the parameter passed. The scaling factor (20 for the real robot or 700 for the simulation) was determined experimentally and may need a minor adjustment based on the speed of your PC, your robot, etc. Notice how the variable **LegoSimulation** is used to set different values depending on whether the program is running in the simulation mode or not. **LegoSimulation** is true only when the simulation library is used. Appendix C discusses this topic further.

Inside the **for**-loop, the distance to the wall is measured and the robot turned to the left or right appropriately. When the loop terminates the robot is halted.

Experimenting

Try experimenting with walls that curve and walls with both inside and outside corners. When you find situations that cause problems, try to develop a better algorithm to make your robot respond more intelligently. You may need to rely on additional sensors (like the bumper) or perhaps periodically look ahead of the robot with the distance sensor. You can also make sharper turns when the robot gets too far from the wall (perhaps because the wall is turning too quickly).

This type of experimentation can be fun and exciting for many people. If you enjoy it, you might consider a career in engineering or programming.

Chapter 7

Dealing with Objects While Following a Line

Previous chapters demonstrated how to avoid objects, follow lines, listen for sounds, and hug walls. Now that you understand how to implement all of these behaviors, it is time to create a program that utilizes all of these skills simultaneously.

Our program will create the environment shown in Figure 7.1. As you can see, it is composed of the line used in previous chapters for line-following, but in this case, there are numerous objects along the line that can block the robot's movement.

The Goal

The goal for the program discussed in this chapter is as follows. The robot should follow the line until it bumps into an object blocking its path. When this happens, the robot should go around the object using the wall-following techniques discussed in Chapter 6. It should do this until it sees the line again. When this happens, the robot should re-acquire the line and start following it again. If a hand clap or other sharp sound is detected during the line following process, the robot should do an about-face and start following the line in the opposite direction.

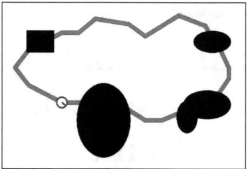

Figure 7.1: This environment will be used for a complex program that utilizes many of the behaviors discussed in previous chapters.

Obviously, the program in this chapter is far more complex than any we have examined so far. If we organize the program properly though, it will be composed of many small modules that perform a simple task each. Such an organization can make writing large programs nearly as easy as small ones. Let's look at the main program (Figure 7.2) to see one method for organizing the program.

The main program begins by including the library and creating the environment shown in Figure 7.1. Notice that the environment is created with a subroutine that does all the work. This means we don't have to concern ourselves (right now) with the details of how this is done.

Next, variables are initialized with the port numbers for the four sensors we will use in this program. We then initialize the robot and the four sensors.

```
Main:
  #include "LegoSimulationLibrary.bas"
  gosub CreateEnvironment:
  SoundPort   = 1
  LinePort    = 2
  RangePort   = 3
  BumperPort  = 4
  call LegoInit(34)
  call LegoRangeInit(RangePort)
  call LegoLineInit(LinePort)
  call LegoBumperInit(BumperPort)
  call LegoSoundInit(SoundPort)
  while true
    gosub FollowLineTillBump
    gosub LegoRetreat
    gosub LegoFaceRight
    gosub FollowWallTillLine
    gosub LegoAdvance
    gosub FindLineAgain
  wend
end
```

Figure 7.2: Just studying this main program can give you a complete overview of how the entire program operates.

Overview of the Algorithm

The while-loop in Figure 7.2 does the real work of the program by calling many modules that handle the details needed for each behavior.

At the beginning of the loop, the subroutine **FollowLineTillBump** will follow a line (this subroutine assumes the robot is currently on a line) until an object is detected with the bumper sensor. When that happens, the subroutine returns and execution continues with the next line in the program, which in this case backs the robot up slightly with the subroutine **LegoRetreat**.

Now that the robot has backed away from the object the subroutine **LegoFaceRight** turns the robot approximately 90° to the right, an appropriate position for using a wall-following behavior to navigate around the object.

The subroutine **FollowWallTillLine** will hug close to the object as it moves forward. During this behavior, it constantly will check the line sensor to see if a line has been found. Once a line is found, this subroutine will return. In order to understand what happens next we need to visualize how the robot will be oriented at this point in time. Try to imagine how the robot will be oriented and then look at Figure 7.3 to see if you are right.

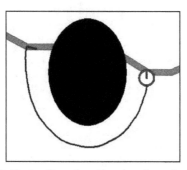

Figure 7.3: Notice how the robot is oriented when a line is encountered during the wall-following behavior.

As you can see from Figure 7.3, when the robot encounters the line after going around an object it will usually be relatively perpendicular to the line. Our goal at this point will be to get the robot to straddle the line facing to the right, thus preparing it for the line-following behavior that will happen as the while-loop starts over.

One easy way of moving the robot to our desired orientation is to move forward half its distance (placing its wheels on the line). This is easily accomplished with the subroutine **LegoAdvance**. Next, we assume we have a subroutine (**FindLineAgain**) that will turn the robot to the right until it finds the line again. Notice this procedure is made up of one routine that is open-loop (advancing) and one that is closed-loop (finding the line again). Notice also that we can handle the inaccuracies of the open-loop movement *because* we follow it with the closed-loop control. The first movement only has to be accurate enough to ensure that all of the line sensors are off the line.

The second movement continues until the line is found, so the robot should be able to accomplish the goal.

Look over the code in Figure 7.2 until you feel confident you totally understand how these actions will accomplish our overall goal. Once you feel confident, we can look into the details of how each of the subroutines used in our main program work. Since we can concentrate on each of them individually, they should not be any more complicated than the programs discussed in previous chapters.

Creating the Environment

One of the subroutines used in our main program was **CreateEnvironment**. It draws the line using a library function, and then uses some RobotBASIC graphic commands to create objects that will block the robot's movements. Figure 7.4 shows the details of this subroutine.

```
CreateEnvironment:
  gosub DrawLine
  Circle 250,250,400,450,black,black
  Circle 550,300,600,380,black,black
  Circle 570,270,700,340,black,black
  Circle 600,100,700,150,black,black
  Rectangle 100,100,170,150,black,black
return
```

Figure 7.4: This subroutine draws the line and objects that block it.

Follow Line Till Object Bumped

Figure 7.5 shows the details of **FollowLineTillBump**. It uses a loop that repeats *until* the bumper sensor is triggered. Inside the loop the line sensor is read and the robot either turns right or left based on whether the line is seen or not.

Next, the sound sensor is checked. If a sound is heard, we use a subroutine called **AboutFace** to make the robot turn 180°. Finally, the status of the bumper sensor is stored in the variable **b** so that it can be tested by the **until** statement.

```
FollowLineTillBump:
   repeat
      call LegoLineSensor(2,a)
      if a=1
        gosub LegoHardRight
      else
        gosub LegoHardLeft
      endif
      call LegoSoundSensor(SoundPort,50,s)
      if s then gosub AboutFace
      call LegoBumperSensor(BumperPort,b)
   until b
return
```

Figure 7.5: This routine follows a line until an object is detected by the bumper sensor.

Follow Wall Till Line Found

The next new routine used by our main program is
FollowWallTillLine. It is shown in Figure 7.6. If the
distance to the wall is very small it takes an easy right.
When the distance is fairly large it takes a hard left to get
back to the wall quickly. For distances in between, the
robot moves slowly toward the wall. These actions
continue until the line sensor sees the line.

```
FollowWallTillLine:
  gosub LegoLookLeft
  repeat
    call LegoRangeSensor(_RangePort,R)
    if R < 8
      gosub LegoEasyRight
    elseif R > 12
      gosub LegoHardLeft
    else
      gosub LegoEasyLeft
    endif
    call LegoLineSensor(_LinePort,L)
  until L
return
```

Figure 7.6: This routine moves around an object until the line is found again.

Finding the Line Again

Recall from the discussion earlier, that the subroutine **FindLineAgain** works by rotating slowly right until the line is detected by the line sensor. Figure 7.7 shows how this is accomplished.

```
FindLineAgain:
  repeat
    call LegoDriveMotors(SLOW,-SLOW)
    call LegoLineSensor(LinePort,s)
  until s
return
```

Figure 7.7: This subroutine rotates the robot right until it finds the line.

About Face

The last new routine, **AboutFace**, is shown in Figure 7.8. It starts by turning right about 90° with **LegoFaceRight** and then using the **FindLineAgain** routine to continue rotating until the line is actually found. If the **LegoFaceRight** is not used first, the second routine would not turn the robot at all, because the line sensor is already on the line. Notice that the **FindLineAgain** routine is the one we used earlier in the main program. The ability to reuse routines is a major advantage of modular programming.

```
AboutFace:
  gosub LegoFaceRight
  gosub FindLineAgain
return
```

Figure 7.8: This subroutine reverses the robot's direction on the line.

Summary

This chapter has demonstrated how small behaviors can be combined to create a larger more intelligent system. Test your skills by modifying the program discussed in this chapter so that it performs differently. Here are some suggested alterations.

❑ Replace the sound sensor with another line sensor so that the line-follow behavior can be smoother.

❑ Replace the bumper sensor with another line sensor so that the line-follow behavior can be smoother. Since you no longer have a bumper sensor, use the distance sensor (looking ahead) to detect objects that block the robot's path.

❑ Make some of the blocking obstacles larger or more irregular to test your robot's ability to circumnavigate around complex objects.

Chapter 8

Line Following with Multiple Sensors

You have learned how to utilize many of the sensors that come with the Lego NXT robot. Purchasing additional sensors allows you to develop more complex algorithms that can improve the intelligence of your robot. For example, you could build a robot with four bumper sensors or four range sensors allowing your robot to detect objects on all four sides.

Lego and other vendors also make other types of sensors that you may wish to consider for your projects. If you develop interface routines for other sensors and wish to share them with other users, please forward them to us and we will consider adding them to the **LegoLibrary** as well as adding support to the **LegoSimulationLibrary**.

Three Line Sensors
In this chapter we will explore the concept of using multiple sensors by creating a three-sensor, line-following algorithm. You could use the previously discussed line-sensor library functions to implement this algorithm, but, in order to make it easier to deal with three sensors we have added special functions to both the `LegoLibrary.bas` and

the `LegoSimulationLibrary.bas`. We will use these functions to show how multi-sensor systems can greatly improve the behavior of your robot.

Developing the Algorithm

In order to develop an appropriate plan for following a line with three sensors, we need to understand the problem. Use a card similar to the one we used in Chapter 3 (see Figure 3.1). The card had only one hole, representing a single line sensor. For this situation, the card should have three holes spaced about the width of a hole apart.

The width of the line that our robot will follow is important. It should be wide enough to cover two adjacent sensors, but not wide enough to cover all three. If you move the card over the surface near a line, there are only eight possible combinations of the sensor readings, as shown in Figure 8.1. The combinations in the figure are made up of 1's and 0's where a 1 indicates a line and a 0 means the absence of one. These eight combinations are the binary equivalent of the decimal numbers shown in the figure.

Move the card over the line and decide what the robot should do for each of the sensor readings. Compare your conclusions with the suggested behaviors in the figure.

Let's look at some of the patterns in Figure 8.1. If the three sensors represent the decimal number 2, for example, it means only the center sensor is *on* indicating that the robot is centered over the line. A reasonable behavior for this condition is for the robot to move forward, perhaps at a fast rate.

If the robot is drifting off the line to the left, we would first see the pattern indicated by a decimal 3. If the robot veers further left, only the right-most sensor will see the line (decimal 1). A reasonable response from the robot for a sensor reading of 3 would be to turn to the right slowly. A reading of 1 should cause the robot to turn right more quickly because the line is far to the right. Using similar reasoning, readings of 6 and 4 should make the robot turn left slightly and turn left quickly.

Decimal	Binary	Suggested Behavior
0	0 0 0	Stop moving (line has been lost)
1	0 0 1	Turn hard to the right (line is far right)
2	0 1 0	Move forward (centered on line)
3	0 1 1	Turn easy to the right (line is right)
4	1 0 0	Turn hard to the left (line is far left)
5	1 0 1	Unlikely pattern, repeat last action
6	1 1 0	Turn easy to the left (line is left)
7	1 1 1	Possible intersection, reverse direction

Figure 8.1: This table of line sensor patterns can help determine the behavior the robot should perform when the pattern occurs.

A reading of 0 means the line has been lost so we might want our robot to just stop when this happens. Alternatively, we might want to do nothing so that the robot will simply continue with its current behavior. Doing nothing actually lets our robot follow much curvier lines because it will continue to veer back to the line even when the line is lost. You can uncomment the `gosub LegoHalt` in Figure 8.2 to compare these two behaviors.

A reading of 5 seems unlikely to occur. Try to imagine how the robot would have to be oriented in order to get such a reading. If this should happen, perhaps the best behavior would be to just do nothing so that the last action taken by the robot will simply continue.

A reading of 7 is also unlikely to occur with a normal line. If our line has some intersections with other lines though, such a reading could come about. When this happens you would have to choose the behavior that makes the most sense for your situation. For our example, let's make the robot reverse its direction if it encounters a line junction.

Coding the Algorithm

Figure 8.2 shows a program that implements the algorithm described by Figure 8.1. It creates the behaviors described above. Notice that the 5th line is commented out so that it does not execute. We will enable this line shortly.

When you run the program the simulated robot will following the line far better than with the algorithm developed back in Chapter 3 (see Figure 3.2). The robot now can handle sharp turns easily without the jerky motion that accompanied the previous algorithm. The improved robot even speeds up slightly when a straight section of line is encountered because we turn the motors on FAST when the robot is centered over the line.

If you uncomment the line near the top of Figure 8.2 you will see a line junction has been added to the robot's environment (see Figure 8.3). When the robot reaches the junction it reads a 7 because all sensors are turned on. Look at the code for this situation in Figure 8.2 to see how it causes the robot to turn around and follow the line in the reverse direction.

Controlling the NXT

The program in Figure 8.2 will control the NXT robot if you change the include file to **LegoLibrary.bas**. The new routines for three line sensors assume that the real robot's line sensors are connected as follows.

> The right line sensor connects to Port 1.
> The middle line sensor connects to Port 2.
> The left line sensor connects to Port 3.

This leaves Port 4 free for any other sensor you would like to experiment with when using this line-following configuration. Chapter 9 offers suggestions for a variety of more advanced projects.

Of course, you do not have to use the same behaviors we chose for each of the sensor readings. For example, you might want your robot to reverse directions when it loses the line.

```
Main:
  #include "LegoLibrary.bas"
  BlueToothPort=34
  gosub DrawLine
  //line 150,70,200,150,15,green
  call LegoInit(BlueToothPort)
  call Lego3LineInit()
  while true
    call Lego3LineSensors(s)
    if s=0
      //gosub LegoHalt
    elseif s=1
      gosub LegoHardRight
    elseif s=2
      call LegoDriveMotors(FAST,FAST)
    elseif s=3
      gosub LegoEasyRight
    elseif s=4
      gosub LegoHardLeft
    elseif s=5
      // should not happen, do nothing
      // which means last action continues
    elseif s=6
      gosub LegoEasyLeft
    elseif s=7
      // could mean a junction, so turn around
      gosub LegoFaceRight
      repeat
        call LegoDriveMotors(SLOW,-SLOW)
        call Lego3LineSensors(s)
      until s&2
    endif
  wend
end
```

Figure 8.2: This program allows the robot to follow a line smoothly and efficiently.

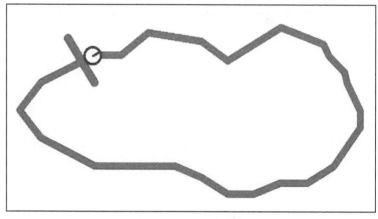

Figure 8.3: When a junction is added to the line the robot turns around and follows the line in the opposite direction.

Developing behavioral algorithms is one of the most exciting aspects of programming a robot. YOU get to decide how your robot will respond to any and all situations. As the programs you write get larger and more complex though, you may be surprised. Often the robot will respond differently than you expect, sometimes making you feel it has more intelligence than you programmed into it. This can happen because the robot will concatenate together sequences of actions based on environmental conditions that you might not have anticipated when your wrote the program. Such unexpected behaviors can sometimes be disastrous, but the robot's response to unanticipated situations can be acceptable or even astonishing, more often than you might imagine.

Chapter 9

Suggestions For Projects

You have learned how to utilize many of the sensors available for the Lego NXT robot and how to use them to create basic behaviors that can be combined to create an intelligent system.

With these skills under your belt, you are ready to create your own algorithms and programs to solve new and interesting problems. Such activities can be stimulating for self-study, but they also make excellent classroom assignments and science projects.

Line Mazes
You can create line mazes and have the robot follow the lines trying to find its way out of the maze or to find an object somewhere in the maze. Your robot would have to be able to detect T-junctions and make choices about which way to turn.

Each junction could be identified by a circular joint large enough to trigger all three line sensors. After finding a junction, the robot could advance, then rotate left and right to find the line again.

You might find that some configuration of four line sensors could help give you more information about the type of junction that the robot has encountered.

Corridor Mazes

You could create a maze of hallways where the walls are actually lines on poster board. The robot could use the line sensors to detect the lines and turn away from them instead of following them.

The robot can look for objects in the maze or try to find its way out. Imagine a contest to see whose robot can find its way out of a cluttered maze in the shortest amount of time.

Grippers

You may rebuild the robot so that the third motor controls some form of hand or gripper. This would allow the robot to pick up objects it finds in a maze and bring them back to the starting point.

Cluttered Rooms

The robot could be programmed to find its way through a cluttered room, perhaps looking for a spot on the floor that can be detected with a line sensor or even a tall block that can be detected by the distance sensor.

Following Lines

This book has provided you the fundamental principles associated with line-following. Consider developing algorithms that allow your robot to follow lines of varying widths and lines that are broken or dotted. To handle such complex situations, your robot will have to adapt its line-following algorithm to its environment by identifying the type of line it is currently following.

Closest Object

Use the distance-measuring sensor to find the object closest to the robot and move to it. If this action was repeated over and over, perhaps the robot could follow a path identified by a series of objects. Imagine a robot that drops objects behind it as it explores a new environment. When the robot has finished its mission, it can follow the trail of objects back to its original position.

Mapping a Room

Allow the user to place the robot at one or more fixed positions in a room. Program the robot to rotate and gather information about the distance to objects around it. Your program could use the data obtained and trigonometry to create an aerial map of where objects are in the room. Since our robot does not have a compass the accuracy will be limited (open-loop timing would have to be used to determine the angles), but this could still be an exciting project for those with a love for mathematics.

More advanced users might use an NXT compatible compass and modify the `LegoLibrary` to interface with it.

Control Over the Internet or With Your Voice

Utilize the principles discussed in our book *Hardware Interfacing with RobotBASIC* to control the Lego robot using verbal commands or over the Internet. You could even combine these two ideas to allow someone speaking in one city to control a robot in another.

Create Your Own Projects

This chapter has given you some ideas to get you started, but we encourage you to dream up your own project ideas. Schools and robot clubs will find that creating contests and challenges can be very motivational. Remember, our library can control multiple bumper and range sensors so let your imagination run wild.

Sharing Your Programs

We invite everyone to send us your programs and a short TXT or DOC file explaining your project. We will post them on our Application or FAQ pages so that others can learn from your work.

Appendix A

Constructing the Robot

O ur robot is composed of many subassemblies similar to those used for the robots shown in Lego's documentation. Utilize these pictures as well as Lego's construction details to duplicate our work or to aid you in creating a robot of your own design. Remember, your robot does not have to be exactly likes ours. The sensor placement should be similar, but the physical appearance can be adjusted to your personal preference.

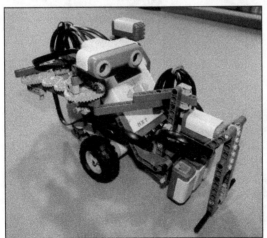

Figure A-1: Our completed robot looks like this.

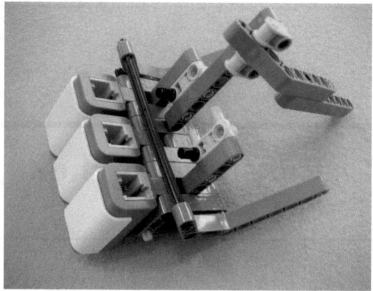

Figure A-2: Three line sensors are mounted side-by-side.

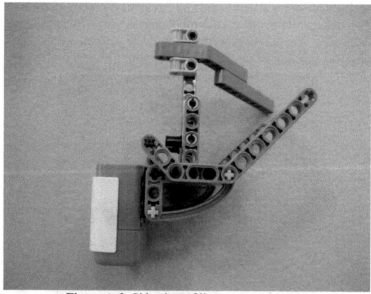

Figure A-3: Side view of line sensor assembly.

Figure A-4: The range sensor is mounted on a sequence of gears.

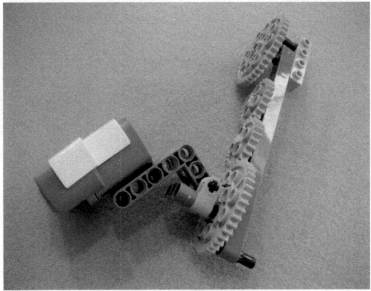

Figure A-5: Side view of range sensor assembly.

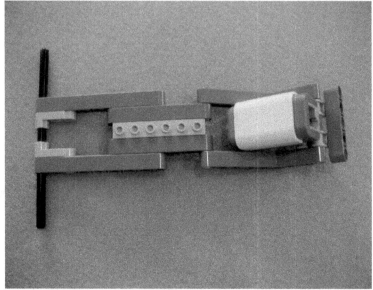

Figure A-6: The front bumper presses a switch sensor.

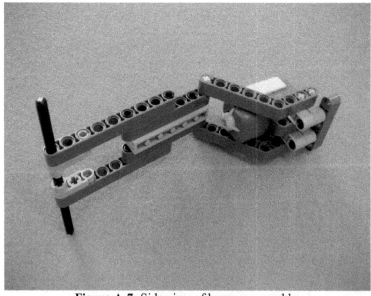

Figure A-7: Side view of bumper assembly.

Figure A-8: The main body of the robot (except for the turret motor) is similar to robots in the Lego documentation.

Figure A-9: Bottom view of the robot's body.

Figure A-10: View of turret motor and mounting for sound sensor.

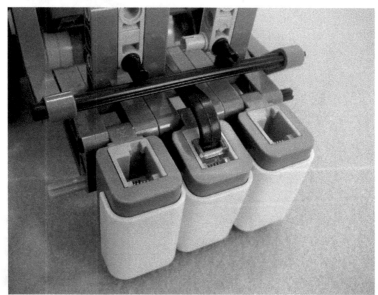

Figure A-11: After the line sensors are mounted, run the cable for the middle sensor as shown. This connection is permanent since it is difficult to move.

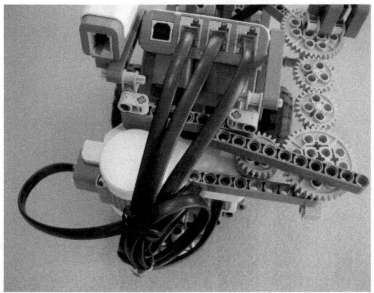

Figure A-12: Use twist-ties to tidy the motor cables. Note the lever arm mounted on the turret motor gear.

Figure A-13: Line sensor cables can be twist-tied to the frame. Note the bumper assembly above the line sensors.

Figure A-13: Opposite side view of line sensors.

Figure A-14: The cable for the range sensor is easily removed for use with other sensors.

Appendix B

The LegoLibrary.bas

This Appendix provides detailed information about the RobotBASIC `LegoLibrary.bas`.

Lego Documentation

Lego provides extensive documentation for those wanting detailed technical information. We have extracted all the information you will need for the projects in this book, but some readers may want more information on what we have done or perhaps even expand on it. You can learn more about Lego's Development Kits (Bluetooth, hardware, and software) by following this link.

http://mindstorms.lego.com/en-us/support/files/default.aspx

Most of what we used comes from the Bluetooth documentation which can be downloaded directly using this link:

http://cache.lego.com/upload/contentTemplating/Mindstor ms2SupportFilesDownloads/otherfiles/downloadFF7F8010 EB6D176857CB6CBF82A8B567.zip

Remember, all the data information you will need for this text is included here. The above links are only given to assist readers who want more technical details and might want to modify our work or expand on it by adding support for additional sensors. Please forward any programs you wish to share with others and we will make them available on our web page.

Direct Commands

In general, the NXT computer can be controlled over a Bluetooth wireless link using specially formatted command strings. Our library functions configure these strings and send them to the NXT robot using RobotBASIC's serial commands.

RobotBASIC captures sensory data being returned by the robot and converts it to useful information that can be obtained with our library functions. For more details, refer to the previously mentioned links to Lego's documentation.

Library Source Code

The complete source code for our **LegoLibrary** is provided below to make it easy for you to view. Don't worry about trying to type the code as the file is included in the downloadable zip file for this book.

> ⓘ The source code for the **LegoSimulationLibrary** is considered proprietary and will not be released at this time. When users share their support for other NXT sensors with us, we will do our best to update the simulation library to handle the new sensors.

```
sub LegoInit(PortNum)
  _LegoSimulation=False
  _FAST = 78
  _SLOW = 70
  _STOP = 0
  _RightTurnTime=900
  _LeftTurnTime=900
  _AdvanceTime=1500
  _DebugTime=120
  _TurretSpeed = 66
  _TurretTime = 900
  _LegoDebug = false
  Dim SS[3]
  SetCommPort PortNum,br115200
return
```

```
//----------------------------------------------------------
sub LegoDriveMotors(A,B)
   //code,code,port,Power,turn on,reg,t ratio,run state
   //,run forever
   SerialOut 12,0,0x80,4,0,A,1,0,0,0x20,0,0,0,0
   SerialOut 12,0,0x80,4,1,B,1,0,0,0x20,0,0,0,0
return




//----------------------------------------------------------
sub LegoThirdMotor(A)
   SerialOut 12,0,0x80,4,2,A,1,0,0,0x20,0,0,0,0
return




//----------------------------------------------------------
sub Wait(t)
  for i= 1 to t
    delay 1
  next
return




//----------------------------------------------------------
sub LegoLineSensor(P,&S)
   if _LegoDebug
     call Wait(_DebugTime)
     gosub LegoHalt
   endif
   SerialOut 3,0,0,7,P-1
   repeat
     CheckSerBuffer NumBytes
   until NumBytes=18
   serin REPLY
   S = (GetStrByte(REPLY,length(REPLY)) !=2)
   if _LegoDebug
     GetLineWidth lw \ LineWidth 1
     rectangle 0,550,799,599,black,white
     xyString 50,570,"Line Sensor (Port ",P,") = ",S
     input "Press ENTER", A
     LineWidth lw
   endif
return
```

```
//----------------------------------------------------------
sub LegoSoundSensor(P,Sensitivity,&S)
   if _LegoDebug
     call Wait(_DebugTime)
     gosub LegoHalt
     GetLineWidth lw \ LineWidth 1
     rectangle 0,550,799,599,black,white
     xyString 50,570,"Sound Sensor: Enter 1 ",\
                "for sound, 0 for no sound."
     input "Type 0 or 1 then Press ENTER", S
     LineWidth lw
   else
     Sensitivity = Limit(Sensitivity,0,150)
     // read sound sensor three times
     for T2= 0 to 2
       // request a read
       SerialOut 3,0,0,7,P-1
       repeat
         CheckSerBuffer T1
       until T1=18
       serin d
       SS[T2]=GetStrByte(d,17)
     next
     // determine if there has been a CHANGE in sound level
     Smax=SS[0] \ Smin=SS[0]
     for T2=1 to 2
       if SS[T2]>Smax then Smax=SS[T2]
       if SS[T2]<Smin then Smin=SS[T2]
     next
     S = ((Smax-Smin) > Sensitivity)
   endif
return


//----------------------------------------------------------
sub LegoBumperSensor(P,&S)
   if _LegoDebug
     call Wait(_DebugTime)
     gosub LegoHalt
   endif
   SerialOut 3,0,0,7,P-1
   repeat
     CheckSerBuffer T1
   until T1=18
   serin d
   S = (GetStrByte(d,15) != 0)
   if _LegoDebug
     GetLineWidth lw \ LineWidth 1
     rectangle 0,550,799,599,black,white
     xyString 50,570,"Bumper Sensor = ",S
     input "Press ENTER", A
     LineWidth lw
   endif
return
```

```
//-----------------------------------------------------
sub LegoRangeSensor(P,&S)
   P--
   if _LegoDebug
     call Wait(_DebugTime)
     gosub LegoHalt
   endif
   SerialOut 7,0,0,0xF,P,2,1,2,0x42
   repeat
      CheckSerBuffer T1
   until T1=5
   serin d
   SerialOut 3,0,0,0x10,P
   repeat
      CheckSerBuffer T1
   until T1=22
   serin d
   S=GetStrByte(d,7)
   S = Round(S/2.25)-5
   if _LegoDebug
     GetLineWidth lw \ LineWidth 1
     rectangle 0,550,799,599,black,white
     xyString 50,570,"Range Sensor = ", S
     input "Press ENTER", A
     LineWidth lw
   endif
return



//-----------------------------------------------------
sub LegoBumperInit(P)
   //               port,switch,boolean
   SerialOut 5,0,0x80,5,P-1,1,0x20
   delay 100
return



//-----------------------------------------------------
sub LegoSoundInit(P)
   //               port,type,mode
   SerialOut 5,0,0x80,5,P-1,0x07,0
   delay 100
return



//-----------------------------------------------------
sub LegoRangeInit(P)
   //               port,ultrasonic,raw
   SerialOut 5,0,0x80,5,P-1,0xb,0
   delay 100
   call LegoRangeSensor(P,S)
   call LegoRangeSensor(P,S)
return
```

```
//----------------------------------------------------------
sub LegoLineInit(P)
   //                      port,light active,raw
   SerialOut 5,0,0x80,5,P-1,5,0
   delay 100
return


//----------------------------------------------------------
sub Lego3LineInit()
   for i=1 to 3
     call LegoLineInit(i)
   next
return


//----------------------------------------------------------
sub Lego3LineSensors(&P)
  P=0
  if _LegoDebug
    call Wait(_DebugTime)
    gosub LegoHalt
  endif
  for i=0 to 2
    SerialOut 3,0,0,7,i
    repeat
      CheckSerBuffer NumBytes
    until NumBytes=18
    serin REPLY
    if GetStrByte(REPLY,Length(REPLY)) !=2 then P+=(1<< i)
  next
  if _LegoDebug
    GetLineWidth lw \ LineWidth 1
    rectangle 0,550,799,599,black,white
    xyString 50,570,"Line Sensors (BIN) = ",Bin(P,3)
    input "Press ENTER", A
    LineWidth lw
  endif
return


//----------------------------------------------------------
sub LegoPen(P)
return


//----------------------------------------------------------
LegoAdvance:
  call LegoDriveMotors(_SLOW, _SLOW)
  call Wait(_AdvanceTime)
  call LegoDriveMotors(_STOP, _STOP)
return
```

```
//--------------------------------------------------------
LegoRetreat:
  call LegoDriveMotors(-_SLOW,-_SLOW)
  call Wait(_AdvanceTime)
  call LegoDriveMotors(_STOP,_STOP)
return


//--------------------------------------------------------
LegoFaceLeft:
  call LegoDriveMotors(-_SLOW,_SLOW)
  call Wait(_LeftTurnTime)
  call LegoDriveMotors(_STOP,_STOP)
return


//--------------------------------------------------------
LegoFaceRight:
  call LegoDriveMotors(_SLOW,-_SLOW)
  call Wait(_RightTurnTime)
  call LegoDriveMotors(_STOP,_STOP)
return


//--------------------------------------------------------
DrawLine:
return


//--------------------------------------------------------
LegoHalt:
  call LegoDriveMotors(_STOP,_STOP)
return


//--------------------------------------------------------
LegoLookLeft:
  call LegoThirdMotor(_TurretSpeed)
  delay _TurretTime
  call LegoThirdMotor(0)
  delay 200
return


//--------------------------------------------------------
LegoLookAhead:
  call LegoThirdMotor(-_TurretSpeed)
  delay _TurretTime
  call LegoThirdMotor(0)
  delay 200
return
```

```
//--------------------------------------------------------
LegoHardRight:
  call LegoDriveMotors(_FAST,_STOP)
return

//--------------------------------------------------------
LegoEasyRight:
  call LegoDriveMotors(_FAST,_SLOW)
return

//--------------------------------------------------------
LegoHardLeft:
  call LegoDriveMotors(_STOP,_FAST)
return

//--------------------------------------------------------
LegoEasyLeft:
  call LegoDriveMotors(_SLOW,_FAST)
return
//--------------------------------------------------------
```

The download file for this book will always have the latest
version of the LegoLibrary.bas. This version has been
included for your convenience.

Appendix C

Calibrating and Customizing LegoLibrary.Bas

Since we provide the full source code for the LegoLibrary (see Appendix B) users can modify it as they see fit. Doing so will make your library unique though, and that can make it difficult to share your programs with others. For that reason, we highly recommend that you always use the latest library available from our web page and modify its behavior using the techniques described in this Appendix.

We expect that most users should *very seldom* need to make the modifications described in this Appendix. If you have a particularly fast or slow computer or if your NXT's motors are unusually slow or fast though, some modifications might be necessary and we want to provide ways to ensure that our libraries can be used under a wide variety of conditions.

Before we examine how to modify the library though, let's look at situations that might make it necessary to do so. We will use a line-following situation as an example.

During a line-following behavior, the robot is constantly moving while the line sensors are being read (and the data obtained is then used to alter the robot's motion). If the robot is moving too fast, it can easily overshoot the line while the sensors are being read thus placing the robot in an unexpected situation (based on previous sensor readings).

There are only two solutions to this problem. The ideal solution is to read the sensors faster, so that the robot can respond to its environment more quickly. Unfortunately, the internal design of the Lego NXT as well as the characteristics of a Bluetooth communication channel prevent increasing the speed of direct control of the robot.

The alternative solution, slowing the robot down, is our only viable option. The robot's speed should be slow enough so that the robot's position over a line will not change significantly between the time the sensors are read and the time the motors actually change their speed or direction. If we make the robot move very slow, there will never be a problem with the robot overshooting the line, but other problems can occur.

If the robot moves too slowly, it becomes easy for it to stall, halting the robot's movement entirely. It is also difficult to get excited about a robot that moves like a snail.

The library routine `LegoInit()` initializes a number of variables (including the speeds indicated by the variables `FAST` and `SLOW`) that can alter the behavior of the NXT robot and/or the simulated robot. The default values in the library were chosen by us through experimentation because they seem to work reasonably well for a wide variety of situations. As you experiment with unique situations and unique environments, you may want your robot to move faster or slower.

It is important for you to realize that changing the values for the speeds `FAST` and `SLOW`, will probably create the need to change other variables. Let's look at a simple example. The `LegoLibrary` contains a routine called

LegoFaceRight that turns the robot approximately 90° to the right. It does this by turning for the amount of time specified by the variable **RightTurnTime**. If you decrease the speed of your robot, you will probably have to increase the turn-time in order to get the same amount of turn.

It is also important to realize that when you change the speed of the real robot that you are not changing the speed of the speed of the simulation (you should NOT, for example, change the values of **FAST** and **SLOW** for the simulation). We have tried to make the simulation respond appropriately, so any modifications you make should be to the standard library, in effect forcing the real robot to act more like the simulation.

The simulation library is reasonably complex, using a variety of interrupt driven routines to control the robot's movements so we will not release the source code for the simulation library. We will try to fix errors reported to us. Also, if any advanced users, develop support for other Lego sensors (and provide that information to us so we can include the routines in the standard library) we will attempt to support the new sensors in the simulation library. Always refer to the current ReadMe file in the download for this book for all the latest information and the most up-to-date version of the library.

The purpose of this Appendix is to help users modify the standard library when it is necessary. As mentioned earlier, in order to make modification as painless as possible we have provided a set of variables that control the robot's behaviors. Refer to the Library Source Code in Appendix B (or preferably to the latest version on our web page) to see the default values for these variables.

These variables, as well as their use in the libraries, are described below. All variables should only be modified AFTER **LegoInit()** has been called, otherwise, the call will reset them to their default values.

When possible, both our real and simulation libraries ignore the value of variables and calls to functions that do not make sense. For example, the simulated robot does not need to initialize its sensors so it simply ignores calls that try to perform this operation.

FAST, SLOW, STOP

These variables are used to control the actual speed of the real robot for the modes indicated by the variable name. The **SLOW** speed is used for open-loop movements, so changing it will generally require that you modify other variables as well (more on this later).

In general, these variables should NOT be modified when the simulation library is being used. The easiest way to comply with this requirement (while still allowing your program to work seamlessly with both libraries) is to utilize the variable **BluetoothPort** (as used in the examples throughout this book) which should have a non-zero value when the real robot is being controlled.

The code fragment below shows how the value of this variable can be use to decide when the variables are to be changed as well as what libraries are included.

```
BluetoothPort = 34  // change to 0 for simulation
if BluetoothPort = 0
    #include "LegoSimulationLibrary.bas"
    call LegoInit(BluetoothPort)
else
    #include "LegoLibrary.bas"
    call LegoInit(BluetoothPort)
    // assign any new values desired for control variables
    FAST = 72
    SLOW = 68
endif
```

You can also use the value of the variable **LegoSimulation** to invoke different actions when different libraries are used. When using this approach you must include the proper library *before* testing the value of **LegoSimulation**. The standard library sets **LegoSimulation** to FALSE, while the simulation library sets it to TRUE. Refer to Figure 6.6 (Chapter 6) for an example program that uses this variable.

`RightTurnTime,LeftTurnTime`
These two variables control how long the real and simulated robots turn when rotating left and right in the routines `LegoFaceRight` and `LegoFaceLeft`. They should be adjusted if your robot is not turning approximately 90°. Two variables are given because your two motors may not respond equally. If you adjust the value of SLOW, you most likely will have to alter the values of these variables.

These variables also control the time used for turns in the simulation mode and may need modifications based on the processor speed of your computer. Use the value of the variable `BluetoothPort` (as described earlier) to make different changes for the real and simulation modes when needed.

`AdvanceTime`
This variable controls the time period that the real and simulated robots Advance or Retreat. Ideally the robot moves ½ its length for both these situations. This means that a robot with its line sensor on a line will advance to where its wheels are on the same line. If you adjust the value of SLOW, you most likely will have to alter the values of this variable.

`DebugTime`
In the debug mode (for both the real and simulated robot), this is the amount of time the motors are allowed to run before being halted (so that sensory information can be displayed). Ideally the robot will move in very small increments so that the robot never overshoots intermediate sensory positions. If your robot is moving too much or too little when debugging, adjust the value of this variable to achieve an appropriate response. If you adjust the value of FAST and SLOW, you most likely will have to alter the values of this variable.

TurretSpeed, TurretTime

These variables control the speed and time used when activating the real turret motor. It is important to use the minimum values possible so that the turret motor will not stall causing unnecessary torque and current.

The Bluetooth Connection

The Lego NXT robot has an integrated Bluetooth transceiver that can be used to communicate with a USB Bluetooth adapter on a PC. Theoretically, any Bluetooth adapter should work, but based on our experience and information on Lego's web pages, compatibility can be an issue. For that reason, we recommend using the Abe adapter available directly from Lego as well as other companies. Figure D-1 shows the Abe adapter.

Figure D-1: Using the Abe Bluetooth adapter ensures compatibility with the Lego NXT robot.

Bluetooth adapters, when used for the first time, must be *paired* in order to establish the connection and setup passwords etc. For many devices this is done automatically but, based on Internet comments from users, many people have trouble utilizing Bluetooth in their projects.

This appendix will share a few tips that do not appear to be in Lego's documentation. They were obtained from Lego's excellent support staff. The information here addresses setting up a single robot for use with a single adapter. Schools or other users that need multiple robots may have to set up individual passwords. Refer to Lego documentation and support for such situations.

In order to establish the Bluetooth connection you will have to setup both the PC and the Lego NXT. Plug the Bluetooth adapter into a USB port on your PC and let it install the DEFAULT Window's drivers. Do NOT install any special drivers that came with your adapter as our experience shows they are often the source of incompatibilities.

Next, instruct the NXT to establish a connection from its end. Ideally you should be able to do this through the menu on the NXT computer itself, but this never seemed to work for us and it was necessary to initially instantiate the connection using the Lego Mindstorm's Software that comes with the Lego NXT. When you install the software and run the Programming Option, you will see a screen similar to Figure D-2. Choose the *Start New Program* option and you will get the programming screen.

On the lower right corner of the programming screen you will see the object shown in Figure D-3. Clicking the top left button on the object will bring up the window shown in Figure D-4.

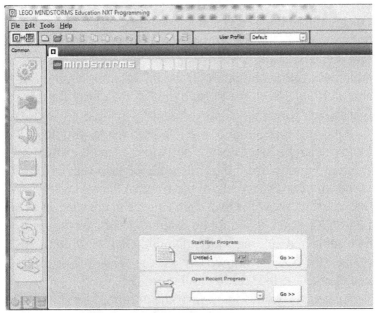

Figure D-2: This is the opening screen for the Mindstorm software.

Figure D-3: These buttons on the programming
screen allows you to access the Bluetooth menu.

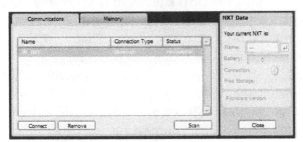

Figure D-4: This NXT Window helps
establish Bluetooth communication.

Once you see the window shown in Figure D-4 choose the SCAN option. Of course, you will need the NXT ready so that it can be found by the scan. Use the NXT menu and Bluetooth and then Search. If the PC is scanning, the NXT should find it. Both the PC and the NXT will ask for a key (password) which is 1234 by default.

Once the basic connection has been made, you no longer need the Mindstorm's software. Open the Bluetooth Devices window from the Bluetooth icon (lower right corner of your PC screen, or the Control Panel) and request that your PC show the available Bluetooth devices. If your Lego NXT is on, it should be listed and a connection will be established automatically. Double-click NXT in the list to open the NXT window. Choose the *Services* Tab and you should see the window in Figure D-5.

As you see from Figure D-5, the port used for the NXT on our machine was 34, which is what is used throughout this book. In general, once all the above has been done ONCE, you do not have to do it again. Just plugging your Bluetooth adapter into your PC and switching on the NXT should automatically establish the connection, and the port number should generally not change.

If all the PC's in a classroom situation have been setup properly, it will be easy for every student to access the robot. Each student can work on their programs using the simulation library and once their program is working the teacher can plug the USB Bluetooth Adapter into their computer. If they substitute our standard LegoLibrary the *same* program they were using for simulation will immediately begin controlling the real robot.

Students can even work on their assignments at home by downloading their own personal free copy of RobotBASIC from www.RobotBASIC.com. RobotBASIC is free for the school too. There are no purchasing costs, no site licenses, and no upgrade fees.

Figure D-5: This Bluetooth window tells you which communication port is used for the connection.

RobotBASIC
Subroutines

M any versions of the BASIC language provide only one kind of subroutine – one called with a **gosub** statement. In general, the variables used in such subroutines are global, that is they are the same variables used throughout the entire program. To clarify this, look at Figure E-1.

```
A = 6
print A
gosub Test
print A
end

Test:
    print A
    A=3
return
```

Figure E-1: An example of a typical BASIC subroutine.

If the program in Figure E-1 is run, it will print as follows:

$$6$$
$$6$$
$$3$$

This shows that the variable A is the same everywhere in the program.

While RobotBASIC supports the standard **gosub** subroutine, it also has a callable function-like routine as demonstrated in Figure E-2. These callable subroutines can be confusing for beginning programmers but they are worth studying because many advanced languages utilize similar capabilities. Because of the educational value as well as the power and flexibility of these new function-style subroutines they will be used, when appropriate, throughout this text. Let's examine some of the attributes available to us when this type of subroutine is used.

```
A = 9
B = 8
C = 7
D = 6
call MyPrint(A, B, C)
print A; B; C; D
end

sub MyPrint(x, y, &z)
    print x; y; z; D
    x = 1
    y = 2
    z = 3
    C = 4
    D = 5
return
```

Figure E-2: RobotBASIC has a function-like subroutine with special attributes.

If you run the program in Figure E-2, it will cause an error because the variable D used in the **MyPrint** subroutine does not exist. If you replace the **print** statement in the **MyPrint** subroutine with the line

```
print x; y; z; _D
```

and run the program you will see the following display.

```
9    8    7    6
9    8    3    6
```

Let's see how these numbers are produced.

First notice that the variables **x** and **y** and **z** take on the values of **A**, **B**, and **C** because they are passed to the subroutine. You see this because the subroutine prints 9, 8 and 7 for these variables. Notice also that the value of **D** is also printed. This is true because the variable **D** is prefixed with the underscore character (_). This tells RobotBASIC that we are referring to the GLOBAL variable **D**, not a variable that is LOCAL to the **sub**-routine.

After variables are printed in the **sub**-routine, they are all assigned new values. When the variables are printed in the main routine though, only the variable **C** has changed. This is true because the variable **z** (in the **MyPrint** parameter list) is prefixed with the **&** character. This tells RobotBASIC to refer to the ORIGINAL variable named in the **call** statement (in this case, the variable **C**) any time **z** is used in the **sub**-routine.

When the variable **D** is changed in the **sub**-routine it does not change the original **D**, but rather creates a new **D** whose value is only valid in the **sub**-routine itself. If the **sub**-routine had modified the value of **_D**, then the original variable **D** would be modified.

> ⓘ For more information on the two types of sub-routines available in RobotBASIC refer to the HELP file as well as a detailed PDF document on this subject available on the FAQ tab at www.RobotBASIC.com.

Appendix F

RobotBASIC Tutorial

This appendix provides a brief introduction to programming with RobotBASIC. It is not intended to provide all the background someone new to programming will need. Refer to the RobotBASIC HELP file or to the beginner's books on our web page for more detailed information.

What is a Program?

A program is simply a set of instructions that allows you to tell a computer what to do. It is not unlike a recipe you would create to tell a person how to cook something.

Suppose you wanted to tell a person how to cook a pound cake. You would give them a step-by-step set of instructions explaining what to do first, what to do next, and so on. A simple computer program is the same.

Computer Languages

You can write the instructions on how to make a pound cake in any language; French or German, for example, instead of English. If you want the person to be able to follow the directions you must use a language they understand. The same applies for a computer program.

The internal design of a computer dictates the language that it can understand. Simple computers, such as the type found in microwave ovens, generally have to be told what to do using cryptic and obscure languages that resemble shorthand. This is necessary because small computers often have limited power and minimal memory.

Today's typical PC, on the other hand, has a huge amount of memory and thousands of times the power of the computers used to put the first men on the moon. Because of this versatility, there have been many languages written for the PC. This book uses a language called RobotBASIC.

RobotBASIC

RobotBASIC is a very powerful language, yet easy to learn. It has all the mathematical capabilities you would expect from any computer language, and even a few seldom found in other systems. It also has many features that make it easy to create exciting simulations and enjoyable video games. It even has an integrated robot simulator that makes it easy to learn how to program a mobile robot.

One of the best things about RobotBASIC is that it is very easy to use. Another advantage is that it is totally FREE. RobotBASIC is a language that is powerful enough to handle complex problems and yet easy to learn and fun to use. You can download your FREE copy of RobotBASIC by visiting the web site:

www.RobotBASIC.com

ⓘ We suggest you download the ZIP file created especially for this book. There are other zip files with many demo programs and files for other books. After you learn the fundamentals about programming with RobotBASIC from this appendix, you can download some of the other zip files and study all the example programs provided in them. The web site provides information for installing everything on your computer so you will be ready to start creating programs.

When you first run RobotBASIC, you will see the screen shown in Figure F.1. View and accept the license agreement, which basically says that you can freely use the program and give it to your friends, but you cannot sell it.

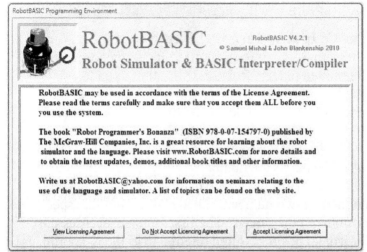

Figure F.1: This is the opening screen for RobotBASIC

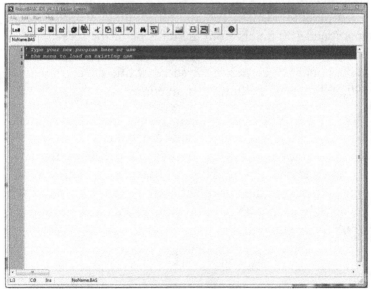

Figure F.2: When you see this screen you are ready to program.

When you accept the license, you will get the screen shown in Figure F.2. Some *comments* are highlighted. They show you where you will type the programs you write. Since these comments are highlighted, the first key you type will replace them. They can also be erased using the **BACKSPACE** key if you wish.

The Output or Terminal Screen

The output screen for RobotBASIC is composed of tiny dots called pixels. RobotBASIC allows you to create graphics on the screen by changing the colors of these pixels. In order to understand the graphics, you need to know how the pixels are organized.

The size of the screen is 800 pixels wide and 600 pixels tall. The pixels are numbered both horizontally and vertically starting with the number zero. Each pixel is defined by two numbers called *coordinates* that specify its position on the screen. The first number specifies the horizontal position (often referred to as the X-coordinate) and the second specifies the vertical position (the Y-coordinate).

A pixel at position 100,200 for example, would be positioned 100 pixels from the left side of the screen and 200 pixels down from the top. The pixel at position 0,0 is at the upper left corner of the screen while the coordinates 799,599 refer to the bottom right corner.

Drawing Lines

RobotBASIC allows you to draw a line on the screen using the `Line` command, which requires you to specify the starting and ending coordinates. The example below will draw a line from the upper-left corner of the screen to the lower-right corner. Notice how the coordinates 0,0 and 799,599 are entered.

```
Line 0,0,799,599
```

Running Programs

In order to see the line actually draw on the screen, we must tell RobotBASIC to run the program. We can do that in several ways. The easiest way is by clicking the ▶ button (the green triangle) at the top of the screen. You could also use the mouse and click the *RUN* menu item at the top of the screen and then click the first option (*Run Program*). If you look carefully at that menu item, you will see it gives you a short cut option (*Ctrl-R*). This means you can also run a program by holding down the *Ctrl* key and pressing the letter R (or r).

Many actions in RobotBASIC can be achieved in a variety of ways. In the future, we will only point out one easy method for doing things. Refer to RobotBASIC's help files (by clicking the ❓ button at the top of the editor screen) to get further information.

If you enter and run the one-line program just discussed, you will get the screen shown in Figure F.3. Notice the line is drawn from the upper-left corner (coordinates 0,0) to the lower-right corner (coordinates 799,599).

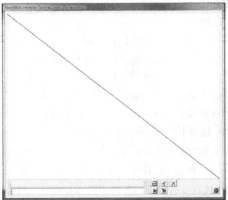

Figure F.3: A line drawn between two corners.

Now that you know how to enter and run a program, let's create something slightly more interesting. Click the ✕ in the top right corner of the output (terminal) screen to close it (returning you to the editor screen), and then type in the lines shown in Figure F.4 (notice our original line is included in the new program. Notice how some letters have been capitalized to make reading easier. The capitalization in this example program is not required, but it is recommended.

```
SetColor RED
LineWidth 3
Line 0,0,799,599
SetColor Green
LineWidth 20
Line 799,0,100,500
End
```

Figure F.4: This program draws two colorful lines.

Let's examine the program in Figure F.4. Each line is executed in turn starting at the beginning and continuing to the last line. The first line sets the color used for drawing to RED. The next line establishes how many pixels wide the drawn lines should be. This means that the line drawn from 0,0 to 799,599 will be red and 3 pixels wide.

The next two lines in the program set the color to green and the width to 10. Notice that these actions only affect future lines drawn, not any lines that have already been drawn. This means the next line in the program draws a wide green line from the upper-right corner of the screen (799,0) to a position near the lower-left corner. The end point (100,500) is positioned 100 pixels from the left and 500 pixels from the top. Run the program to see the results.

Notice the last line in the program is an END statement. It tells the program to quit. In this particular case, the program will stop even if you did not have an END because there are no more lines to execute. If you add lines after the END statement, they will not execute.

Saving and Retrieving Programs
You can save your programs at any time using the *SAVE* option in the *FILE* menu. This allows you retrieve the

program later using the *OPEN* option. You should get into the habit of saving your programs often and definitely before you run them. This will ensure that you do not lose all your hard work if the computer crashes for some reason.

Errors in a Program

If you make a typing mistake in a program the computer may not be able to understand what you want it to do. When you run a program that has errors of any kind, RobotBASIC will alert you with an error message. If in the program of Figure F.4, for example, you wrongly spell `LineWidth` as `LinWidth` then running the program will create the error shown in Figure F.5.

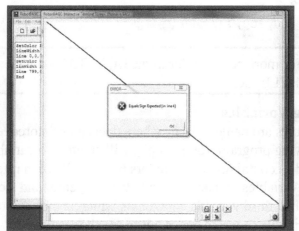

Figure F.5: RobotBASIC tells you when it finds an error.

Notice that the program drew the red line, since the error did not occur until after that point in the program. The error message in this case (**Equals Sign Expected**) will mean more to you after you gain experience with programming. RobotBASIC cannot always identify what is wrong with a line, but it will point you to the offending position in the program. When using this introductory text, most of your errors are most likely caused by simple typos.

Adding to the Program

Suppose we want to draw a line from the center of the screen horizontally to the right edge of the screen. The center of the screen should be at 400,300 because the entire screen is 800 wide and 600 tall. If we want the ending point to be the right edge of the screen, then the X-coordinate should be 799 and the Y-coordinate needs to be the same as the Y-coordinate for the starting point, or 300 (to ensure that the line is horizontal). Add the following line just before the END statement in Figure F.4 and run the program again. Can you predict what color the line will be? Can you change the line so it is 5 pixels wide and BLUE?

```
Line 400,300,799,300
```

> ⓘ For more colors, refer to the CONSTANTS page of the HELP file.

Using Variables

Variables are named places where data can be stored. The following program, for example, will create two variables (**A** and **b**) containing the numbers 6 and 7. We can refer to those variables by name and add them together and store them in a third variable called **cat**, which is then printed. Type in this program and run it to see the results.

When using variables it is important to use the correct spelling and capitalization. The variables **B** and **b**, for example are two different variables.

```
A = 6
b = 7
cat = A+b
print cat
```

Using Loops

RobotBASIC has several different kinds of loops (**For-Next**, **While-Wend**, and **Repeat-Until**) all of which are detailed in the RobotBASIC Help File. The program below demonstrates a FOR-loop. It causes the variable **x** to assume the values of 1 through 10. This means that the first time through the loop, **x** will be 1, the second time it will be 2 and so on. Run the program to see what is printed.

```
for x = 1 to 10
  print x
next
end
```

Making Decisions

Decisions can be made in programs using an IF-statement. RobotBASIC has several types of IF-statements (**if-then**, **if-else-endif**, and **if-elseif-else-endif**), but a simple example is shown below. It prints the numbers from 1 to 4 in red and the others in green.

```
for x = 1 to 10
  if x<5
    SetColor RED
  else
    SetColor GREEN
  endif
  print x
next
end
```

More Help

Remember, this Appendix is only intended to be a brief introduction to programming with RobotBASIC. If you need more help, refer to the RobotBASIC HELP file or some of the beginner's books available on our web page.

Index

www.ingramcontent.com/pod-product-compliance
Lightning Source LLC
Chambersburg PA
CBHW071223050326
40689CB00011B/2437